The Cyclothymic
Student

## A GUIDE FOR ASSESSMENT
## AND INTERVENTION

John A. Paulus PhD

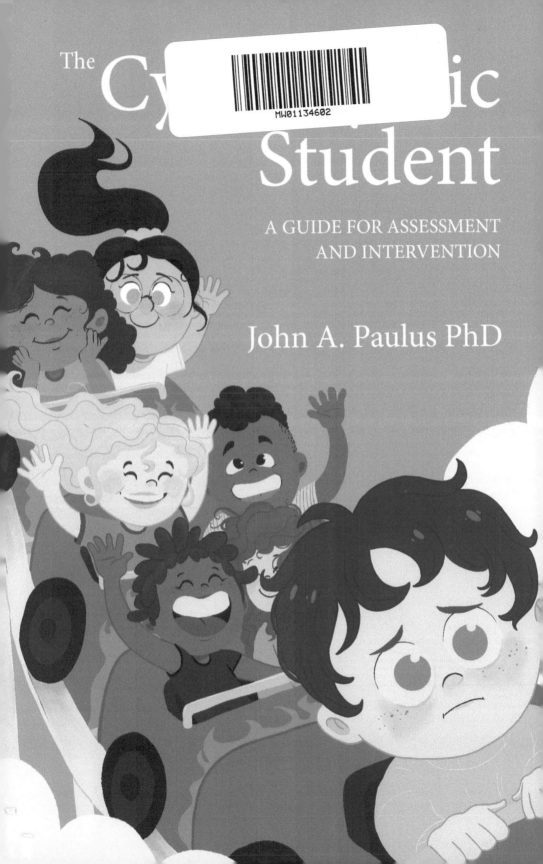

# The Cyclothymic Student

John A. Paulus PhD

Illustrations on cover and title page created
and designed by Seven K Bury
Ms. Bury is a graduate of Columbus College
of Art and Design (CCAD)

# CONTENTS

# INTRODUCTION

Thank God for good dentists! I went to see Dr. Mary K for my 6-month checkup during November 2018 and she found an area of inflammation in my upper jaw. By February of 2019 I had 3 surgeries and a hole in my upper jaw and cancer removed. During the next six months I saw a dentist at the Cancer Hospital dental clinic to construct an "obturator" to cover the hole in my upper jaw. My dentists with their acute observation and caring referrals saved my life.

## Children and Suicide

Over those same two years, 2018 and 2019, some children with mental health problems were not so lucky with their lives. On May 2018, 10-year- old Ricky committed suicide in Ohio while his family had gone to a baseball game. Ricky had shown mood changes and had been fighting at school and using bad language. * Note: real names are not used in this book to protect privacy of families.

Ricky had two family members commit suicide during the past 20 years. Even with the red flags and signs of a serious mood disorder, his community and his counselors may have overlooked diagnostic signs of a 'mood swing disorder'. His mother wanted his story in the newspaper to tell others about this danger. Chapter 9 explains why taking family mood history is so crucial in treating young people with behavioral problems and mood swings.

The Akron Beacon Journal article reported suicide by children is a growing problem. "Although state data on the deaths of Ohioans in 2017 is still incomplete, the Ohio Department of Health had recorded by March 111 suicides of young Ohioans during 2017." "Eighty-nine of the victims were

15 to 19 years old, twenty-one were ages 10 to 14, and one was younger than 10." These tragic events are a bad deal for these children. I believe inadequate assessment of mood and sleep disorders in children, a lack of accurate diagnoses, and marginal mental health treatment takes center stage in this sad course of events.

Effective education and training of school staff and parents may help them identify signs and symptoms of mood disorders, sleep disorders, and related at-risk behaviors. Such training will point out risk of suicide, related bizarre and emotionally disturbed thinking, and possible threat to others, as linked to mood and sleep disorders in children. Mental health providers need additional training in this complex area as well. Too frequently these disorders are misdiagnosed and overlooked. Too often they are labeled as an ADHD, disruptive behavior disorder, or an Impulse disorder.

When I saw the newspaper article on 12-year-old Darren's suicide, alarm bells went off. "I need to finish writing a book on a Cyclothymic Disorder, a guide to help parents, school personnel, and mental health clinicians identify children at risk." This book can alert adults and caretakers about children at risk for mood swing problems, aggressive behavior and suicide.

There are stressful events that encourage depression and self-destructive behavior. Depression, severe emotional stress and mood changes may cause suicide. On Monday, July 2019, an article in the newspaper stated: *Grandma inspired to help after boy's suicide.* When Diana of Smalltown, Ohio lost her 12- year- old grandson, Darren to suicide in March, she began to manage her grief by joining the 'Don't Give Up Movement'. Diana began to plant signs in yards that said: "You are Worthy of Love", "You Matter", and "Don't Give Up".

This grandmother changed her thinking and behavior to help others with depression and mood disorders. She wanted to help youth in need of acceptance and support. She moved from passive, not knowing what- to-do behavior to telling herself: "Do something." She summed up her new behavior by saying: "We're meant to love everyone."

## Mood Disorders Disrupt Learning and Sleep

This guide describes how mood enters the interplay of day- to- day life pressures of teens and children. Mood swings and cycling play a large role in the disruption of learning, in the failure to develop social skills, and they discourage the learning of vocational and academic skills. Chapter 1: *How A Mood Disorder Disrupts Learning* provides examples of students with Cyclothymic Disorder having difficulty with spelling, reading, and other academic subjects. When young people have changing moods, they grow in **"self-doubt" and lose motivation** to learn and they decline in their ability to grow in confidence and independence.

One mood disorder, Cyclothymic disorder, plays a key role in causing difficulty for young people in school settings, in peer relations, and in career growth. A Cyclothymic disorder is a mood-sleep disorder that blocks learning, dampens motivation, encourages distractibility, and discourages friendship making and social skills. Chapter 3: *Susie Lacks Sleep* describes how loss of sleep and sleep deprivation caused by Cyclothymic Disorder needs assessment and treatment to prevent disruption in the lives of these students. Sleep loss causes learning problems and relationship problems.

## Loss of Control of Mood and Behavior

Cyclothymic disorder, a neuro-biological disorder, is a mild to moderate form of manic-depressive illness or bipolar disorder. Cyclothymic Disorder is diagnosed by such clinical symptoms and signs as changing periods of depressed mood, and excitable, energetic, nervous, irritable, aggressive mood. Chapter 9: *Suicidal Depression and Effective Intervention* reviews case examples and research showing the impact of Cyclothymic Disorder. This mood disorder has rapid mood changes from hypomanic mood to moderate and severe depression that encourage suicidal thinking and behavior. These mood changes encourage a loss of control.

## Good Nutrition Makes a Difference

The encouraging and exciting news is that there are effective, new treatments for Cyclothymic disorder that can change the lives of young people. They create the opportunity for a better future. Chapter 7: *Nutrition for a Healthy Mind and Body* reviews research from nutritional experts during the past 20 years. They provide families guidance on improving the health, mood, energy, vitality and weight of their children and teenagers.

## Alternative Treatments

Social skills training, parent and peer counseling groups have been used at the Ohio State University and other universities to help children and families cope with bipolar spectrum disorders. Yet many mood disordered children prefer effective individual therapy along with play therapy to manage anxiety and nervous mood. These treatments can provide direction to families in coping with the challenges and hardships of mood disorders, sleep disturbance, and related conflicts and stressors.

The future for treating mood disorders, drug abuse and suicide in young people is promising. Therapists and teachers can encourage, educate, motivate children, teenagers, and their families to learn about mood disorders, so that they can learn more quickly how to manage these disorders. They may learn about effective treatment and how to help their peers with depression and mood swings. In this way we can learn to prevent serious mental health problems and create brighter futures for our children.

John A. Paulus, Ph.D

8/12/2020

# Chapter 1

# How A Mood Disorder
# Disrupts Learning

---

Cyclothymic Disorder is a biological illness which frustrates some children and teenagers. Students with this mood disorder find it hard to concentrate and focus on their schoolwork. Reading and writing become a big chore. The cyclothymic student may avoid the classroom so academic tasks need not be faced.

## Restless Mood, Restless Behavior

A cyclothymic disordered child or teen may look like a young person on the move. Jeremy, age 10, for example, is hyperactive and, he can't stop moving nor sit still in the classroom. He reads in a rapid, skimming fashion and is only able to read a page or two. Soon he needs to go back and reread what he read moments before. He forgets what he reads. At home, he finds it difficult to sit still at the dining table while Mom or Dad scold him for moving and chewing his food rapidly.

Jeremy has hypomanic, restless mood and is unable to sit still while at school. He has a hard time listening to the teacher for longer than five minutes. His mind moves quickly from one thought to another and has already moved on to the next subject of interest. Thoughts are whirling through his mind: "What are Charley and I doing after school? I wish we could look for some Marvel comics. Maybe we could go to the Game Box store and pick up a game." "I wish I didn't have to sit here and be bored". When Jeremy has a hard time listening, he may learn only half of what he is instructed. He earns C's or lower grades in school.

Ricky, age 9, makes many math errors and skips over problem-solving steps. We sent a letter to his doctor to treat his energetic mood. When treated with a low dose of Lithium carbonate, a mood stabilization medication, *he was able to slow down, check his work and correct his errors* when he worked on math problems. With his new mood medication he was no longer excitable, had calm mood, and completed school work.

**Anxious, worrisome, sad, hopeless feelings are often present**

Shelley, a fifth grader, is worried. She received bad grades on the last two math tests and her mother tells her to study more or ask for more help at school. Mom yells at her when she is up past 9 p.m. doing homework. She is feeling sad, squeezed, pressured, and hopeless. "It's never going to get better for me." "I will always be stupid at math and the others will make fun of me". These thoughts represent Sharon's mood and feelings as her thoughts go from sad, nervous, to being tense, agitated, and upset.

Teachers see that these students possess similar qualities. They can't concentrate, are unable to listen, are restless or disruptive, or may be quiet and withdrawn. They may not do well in reading, spelling, math or writing.

**Many Cyclothymic Students are Smart, Yet Get Tripped Up by this Distracting Mood:**

Last year a mother brought in her bright middle school daughter Carol, who had *great difficulty with spelling.* Carol reported: "I can't remember spelling words." Her mother commented: "A week later she forgets them." Carol added in a sad tone: "All my school years I have had spelling problems." Her mother stated that she has trouble sitting still. She had earned A's and B's in school. Carol's mother completed the CPRS-48, a Conner's rating scale and rated her as having excitable, impulsive mood, being restless and always up and on the go, and having stomach aches much of the time. She rated Carol as having problems with sleep very much of the time.

On the Paulus Mood Inventory (PMI) she reported her daughter as being bossy, being distractible and losing focus, tossing around and talking during her sleep. Carol had complaints of being tired and bored at school. Her mother rated Carol as having sudden changes in mood, being loud and talking fast, getting angry easily and becoming nervous.

On a sleep questionnaire, Carol, age 11, reported that she is bothered by restless and fitful sleep, poor quality of sleep, and that her sleep is not restful no matter how much sleep she gets. (Chapter 3 goes into detail about types of sleep problems). Carol and her mother worked out a treatment plan with me to address her spelling problem and lack of confidence with this skill. She and this psychologist worked with a 5th Grade Master Spelling List (Copyright @ 2011 K12Reader.com). We began with Week 1: Sight words, suffix – ant and academic vocabulary.

When this psychologist asked Carol to read spelling words out loud, she read too rapidly. As we practiced the spelling test and went back over the 50 percent of her misspelled words to correct them, we found her rushing through her correction work. She wrote: *'quite'* for quiet, *'imagrint'* for immigrant, and *'ignerent'*, for ignorant. She knew enough to get the general structure of the words correct.

This psychologist saw her writing words so quickly that she was not able to listen to the sounds of each syllable, each portion, or vowel. She had to learn to slow down, exaggerate the syllables or parts of the word and each e, a, i, o, or u. Dr. (J) Paulus asked her to slow down and break words into syllables while she wrote them. Dr. JP challenged her: "See how slow you can go."

She expressed doubt and stated: "I'm not good at spelling." Like a young colt, she wanted to finish the race quickly. This psychologist encouraged her: "See how slow you can go. We need to practice breaking down the words into syllables, and you will improve your spelling." We clowned around and exaggerated the syllable and vowel sounds so she could see how to sound out the words before she wrote them. She began to improve her spelling gradually over several sessions.

We completed further assessment and testing, and Carol's mother completed child behavior checklists for home and school. This provider was interested to find out what contributed to her spelling problems. She had earned high grades in all other subjects.

Carol reported that she disliked school except for science and history. She disliked socializing with peers, yet she flourished and did well in theatre with motor activity, action, and guided emotional expression. She talked excitedly and with enthusiasm about being a performer in her theater group. She reported she had no problems remembering her lines. Poor sleep patterns, difficulty getting up in the mornings, and periods of temperamental mood had been problems for her during the last year. This examiner believed she had a mood and sleep disorder.

Her mother requested a report for school that would guide personnel in creating a helpful IEP. This psychologist requested her mother to send him key words, concerns, recommendations that she would like to see included in this school intervention plan. This psychologist crafted a report that spelled out the need to evaluate this young lady for a gifted program, to accommodate her sleep disorder and related distractibility, and to help her manage her anxious, nervous mood. Dr JP suggested they provide supportive help with her spelling and more hands-on school assignments that permitted periodic movement.

Her parents appreciated the help this psychologist provided their daughter in improving her spelling skills. However, they were not ready to address her mood disorder or Cyclothymic disorder problems at that time. Dr. Paulus gave them a written report and recommendations for later use by their family/child psychiatrist.

## Looks Like ADHD, But It is a Different Kind of Brain, Neurological Disorder.

Cyclothymic Disorder, a restless mood/behavior disorder, is easily confused with ADHD. These two disorders share some common symptoms and they also have unique differences. Dr. Charles Popper wrote: "All of the features of ADHD can be seen in mood disorders at times, so ADHD is a diagnosis reached only after ruling out a mood disorder." Popper C., (1996).

While children with ADHD may calm down from a temper tantrum in twenty minutes, Dr. Popper observed that bipolar disorder or mood disordered children may be angry up to four hours. He observed that children with ADHD do not generally show depression and tend to arouse quickly in the morning. Dr. Popper observed that "irritability is common in children with mood disorders".

**Key Signs and Symptoms of Cyclothymic Disorder:**

This mood disorder has several key signs and symptoms:

- **Restless, hyperactive behavior.**
  Parents and teachers may say that these kids will not sit still, do not want to sit quietly, or are oppositional. That is not accurate. The truth is that these young people do want to sit still, be calm and cooperative. Yet their restless nature and biology do not permit them to be this way. We now know that these students have *a neurobiological condition* that revs up their minds, bodies and mouths.

- **Restless mind with racing thoughts and distractibility.**
  From 2000 to 2012 this individual had the privilege of working as a psychologist at a university behavioral health center. This provider worked with public school students and college students referred for psychological evaluations. Often these students were referred by the office of disability services to determine whether they had ADHD, a learning disorder, or other diagnoses that interfered with learning. The students and student athletes were under performing and not achieving like their peers in class.

  With structured diagnostic interviews, ADHD testing, memory testing, achievement testing, and mood and anxiety inventories, we were able to arrive most of the time at diagnoses. Diagnoses varied from ADHD, to mood disorders, sleep disorders, and specific learning disorders.

Some college and high school students observed that they had great difficulty with reading comprehension and had to re-read paragraphs several times to remember important ideas. They shared that they read so quickly that they skipped over material. In addition, they reported that their minds were so active and were thinking of other things and only heard part of the professor's lecture. Some could identify how rapidly their minds worked and stated: "My mind is going 100 miles per hour."

Conversely, some students daydreamed for periods of time, looked outside or looked at what other students are doing. They thought about what they wanted to do today, what sport and activity is next, or what they wanted to do when they got home.

- **Learning Problems are common:**
  Parents and students complained that while the school year started well, it became difficult to keep up good grades and motivation as the school year progressed. University students told me they did well in the fall and were motivated to study. But by winter, they lost motivation, energy, and became increasingly distracted, depressed, or frustrated.

Over the past 20 years this psychologist worked with a several high school and middle school students who had school phobia and school refusal problems. We might think that many of these students were below average intelligence, but that was not the case. Many of these students fought with mood, sleep problems, distractibility, nervousness, hypomanic mood and social anxiety.

Approximately half of students seen in our university clinic had learning disabilities related to these neurobiological/ mental health problems. Reading comprehension problems were often linked to distractibility and racing thoughts and frequently related to a mood or sleep disorder. Some of these college aged students with reading and spelling problems were found to have problems with impulsive, nervous, or hypomanic mood.

This evaluator referred several college age students and some younger students for treatment, and the psychiatrists stated that "these students had ADHD." He would see patients and their parents a few months later and they were discouraged with treatment. They were frustrated. Was it possible that some child psychiatrists did not make the connection between mood disorders, sleep disorders, mental health disorders and learning disorders?

- **Sleep Problems.**
  Sleep problems are a key to mood, distractibility disorders, and have a powerful effect on children and teenagers. It effects their school performance, their peer relationships, as well as their home life. Disturbed sleep, erratic sleep with repeated awakenings, and difficulty falling asleep with an overly active mind are key indicators that a *Cyclothymic mood disorder* or another mood disorder may be present.

  This provider often tells clients and students that a Cyclothymic Disorder looks like an attention-distractibility disorder with extra wrapping or clothing. You can add irritable mood, restless or excitable mood, and disturbed sleep with related fatigue, sleepiness, and learning problems *to this distractibility disorder.* It is not surprising that these students have behavior problems in school and often fall behind their peers in academic achievement. Consequently, they experience pressure from parents and teachers to get on medication "to make our (adult) lives easier!"

- **Mood changes.**
  Parents, teachers, and other professionals know that many students with mood disorders and other mental health disorders face difficulty and challenges within the school setting. When you are

shy, the bully comes looking for you. When you lack friends or size other students may pick on you. When students deal with mood swings it is difficult to manage relations with others in a calm and confident manner and to focus on schoolwork.

Students with learning, mood and anxiety difficulties told me that they lose confidence in class work and they dislike school. They begin to talk to parents and their counselors about attending an online school. Some parents find it less trouble to home school their children than to push them each morning to go to school.

## Burdens and Challenges:

Children and teenagers with Cyclothymic Disorder have extra burdens at school and these burdens include such things as:

1. Fear of losing control of emotions or temper._Moods change quickly at home and school. These mood changes can happen automatically with a neurochemical change in the brain. Mood can change when a teacher requests work and the child or teen is tired from erratic, restless, poor sleep. A teenager can have a mood change when a peer asks a question and be irritable for no reason. Yet there are explanations for this irritable mood. (See the next chapters).
2. With Cyclothymic Disorder the student is so distractible they hear part of what the teacher is saying and instructing; and they miss information, directions for an exam, and what to do for their assignment.
3. These young people become nervous, restless, scared, tense, and anxious in class. Cyclothymic youth can have panic attacks and may suddenly get sick to their stomachs or have a severe headache. With this neurobiological disorder, excitable, nervous mood, or shy, avoidant, depressed feelings make it hard for this young person to talk to peers, to approach them, listen to them, and engage them in conversation.

4. *Being restless* is a big problem at school. Students are supposed to sit still. However, sitting still is a torture for these young people. Fortunately, today some schools are realizing these difficulties and they are adding key tools to the environment including desks with 'rocking bars' for restless feet, 'manipulative items or tools' in the classroom, and stationary bicycles in the hallways. Now these restless, nervous students have a better chance of coping and succeeding in the school setting. (In Chapter 10 we examine other hands-on tools for these restless students).

5. Cyclothymic children and teenagers can be argumentative, and they dislike being told what to do. Many of these children are bright, "already know" many things, and have an attitude stating: "you don't need tell me what to do." Some of their parents may have similar temperaments.

6. *It is common* for cyclothymic children and teenagers to be obsessive-compulsive, perfectionistic, and work slowly on exams and papers for fear of making mistakes. Whenever this provider administered the Woodcock Johnson Tests of Achievement to school students, and the Nelson-Denny Reading Test to college students, these anxious, perfectionistic, Cyclothymic students took much longer to complete a reading test than an average reader their age.

**Accommodations:**

Schools and colleges are required to make accommodations and allowances for Mood Disordered and distractible young people through HR 4303B. Many of these nervous, perfectionistic students are fearful of making mistakes. We need to provide flexible testing times and non-distracting environments to encourage cyclothymic, mood disordered students when they take their exams. Such students need extra encouragement as they may be hard on themselves and judge themselves in demanding ways. They need our acceptance, not our judgment.

**Summary:**

Cyclothymic Disorder is a mood disorder which stokes up embers and flames of feelings, mood swings, irritability, nervous tension and scattered, racing thoughts. These changing moods, feelings, bodily sensations, and erratic thoughts disrupt and distract these mood disordered students from concentrating, from learning and listening. Learning is difficult with this biological, genetic illness.

To treat this complex mood disorder, a variety of treatment approaches at school and at home are needed. Treatment with physicians, psychiatrists, therapists, school intervention team members and group counselors are needed. This book covers a variety of topics, assessment and treatment approaches that address how children and teens manage this Cyclothymic Disorder. We will examine how these mood disordered students can learn to relate better to peers and family members, and patiently learn emotional coping skills and work skills.

# Chapter 2

# Larry, A Troubled Third Grader

---

## Introduction

A Cyclothymic Disorder, a 'mixed mood disorder' often encourages concentration and behavior problems. This mood disorder encourages an elementary student to be distractible, moody, and to be disruptive. Cyclothymic students have restless minds and bodies. They have difficulty focusing on schoolwork when their minds and bodies are eager to move elsewhere and their minds are excitable. Parents and teachers may be aware that these children often have poor sleep patterns and are not well rested. They will likely be irritable the following school day.

## A Case Example of a Cyclothymic Elementary School Student

When this mental health provider first saw Larry, age 9, he commented: "I may be talking at school too much. Making smart remarks." Larry knew he was disruptive in class, wanted attention, but rarely received positive attention. His mother reported that "Larry has a problem concentrating when talking to others" and, "he'll focus everywhere else". She commented that: "He is constantly moving and talking too much." He interrupted his mother frequently when she talked to me about him.

We reviewed his background, his family and developmental history. Larry's mother reported he had a good weight of 10 pounds at birth and good health with normal development. She reported that her mother's family had no learning problems, her half-brother had problems learning, and her maternal aunt had a problem with "nerves" and depression.

## Learning, Frustration and Anger Control Problems
## are Common for the Cyclothymic Student

Larry is an obese third grader who weighs 145 pounds. He sees his treating psychiatrist regularly for treatment of his ADHD and she prescribed him 30mg., Ritalin, two times daily. His psychiatrist referred Larry for a psychological evaluation and cognitive behavior therapy. On a behavioral form, his mother reported that Larry has a hard time getting along with others, has trouble keeping friends, and trouble learning. She reported he has behavioral problems at school and often has difficulty controlling frustration and anger. His treating psychiatrist changed his medication to Adderal, a psychostimulant, because Ritalin was not effective. She explained to the mother that this drug can be addictive and requires a new prescription each month. This medication could cause high blood pressure and a rapid heart rate.

Larry's mother completed a child behavior checklist (CBCL for Ages 4 to 18) and reported that Larry's reading, language arts, social studies, and science grades were below average. His math achievement was average. On this behavior checklist she reported that her son argues a lot, can't concentrate for long, is hyperactive, and is disobedient at school. His mother reported that he is mean to others, may destroy his things, and acts impulsively. These behaviors and signs_may describe students with Cyclothymic disorder.

Larry's mood symptoms, such as becoming easily embarrassed, clowning around, talking loud, and suddenly becoming irritable and angry, typify a child with Cyclothymic disorder. His teacher reported that Larry was at grade level with his oral language (may indicate an average IQ), yet he is still far below grade level in his writing, reading comprehension, math, and spelling. Mood changes, poor ability to focus, being argumentative is typical.

This underachievement typifies elementary and middle school students with distractibility and mood disorder symptoms including youth who have mixed mood symptoms. *Cyclothymic children usually have a mixture* of being restless, irritable, unmotivated, fatigued, and lacking in concentration. Unless their mood is agreeable, and they receive proper medical treatment and nutritional planning, there may be little success in motivating these students. (See figure 1).

Larry's teacher expressed concern that he speaks out constantly and is very aggressive towards others. She reported that Larry acts too young for his age, makes odd noises, argues a lot, and fails to finish things. She further reported that Terry is restless, acts confused, behaves cruelly toward others, and gets into many fights.

His problems at school are so numerous and severe that it is unlikely that he has an ADHD disorder. Parent and teacher reports suggest a mood disorder. Often doctors and parents dislike labeling elementary school age children as having a mood disorder. They see it as a negative label and that others will judge this young person. There is an *obvious need* to educate everyone regarding this medical disorder and that a description of a mood disorder will be helpful towards treatment, intervention, and helping these students be successful in life.

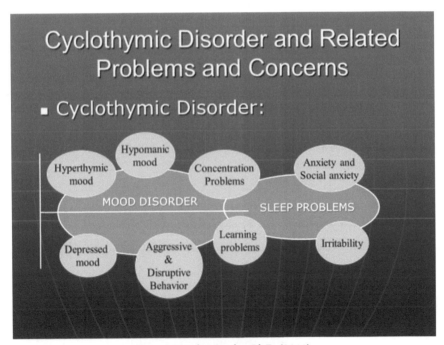

Figure 1: John Paulus PhD (2010)

Larry's behaviors, mood changes, and his school adjustment problems are well explained by the information on Cyclothymic Disorder described in *Figure 1* and *Figure 2 (created, designed by J Paulus)*. Research articles in Chapter 9 detail the mixed mood picture, the tendency toward health problems and complaints. Rapid changes can occur such as having depressive, unmotivated, avoidant mood to changing to irritable, angry, wound-up, hypomanic, aggressive mood with swings in energy and appetite.

What is hypomanic mood? Children with hypomanic mood may be energetic and very restless, are not able to sit still, may be grouchy or irritable and may argue with others. They may also have racing thoughts. These students are not able to listen to parents or teachers because their minds are off to the races and "miles down the road", way ahead of everybody else.

**Students with hypomanic mood have difficulty with the following demands and situations at school. Following are some of the traits and behaviors:**

- difficulty paying attention to what the speaker says or to directions
- easily distracted in the classroom
- find it hard to sit still
- noise, talking, or movement in the classroom are distracting and may be irritating to them.
- have difficulty focusing on one subject or taking on a problem one step at a time.
- easily bored and being unable to wait to get to the next activity
- may be impatient and easily angered
- may argue with others or get into fights
- can't manage mood changes (when not on an anticonvulsant / mood stabilizing medication)

Hypomanic mood is the "up", energetic, excitable mood that parents will see over the different seasons of the year and may see day to day as well. It's also a nervous, anxious mood that encourages "hurry-up" behavior': 'we have to get this job or task done quickly so we don't look stupid or slow.' It is the thrill of the start of a roller coaster ride, where depressive mood is the end of fun. Reading and arithmetic homework quickly become tedious.

*Figure 2* lists some of the problems and consequences of environmental pressures on the Cyclothymic child and teenager.

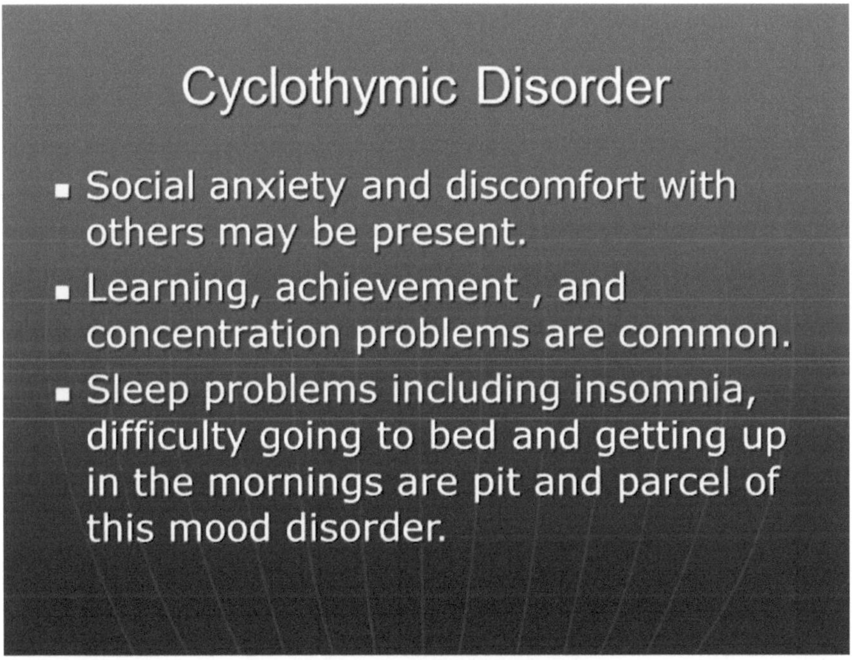

## Cyclothymic Disorder

- Social anxiety and discomfort with others may be present.
- Learning, achievement , and concentration problems are common.
- Sleep problems including insomnia, difficulty going to bed and getting up in the mornings are pit and parcel of this mood disorder.

Figure 2 John Paulus Ph.D (2011)

My evaluation of "Larry" was conducted over 15 years ago and psychiatrists hesitated and resisted the idea of prescribing a mood stabilizer, or anticonvulsant medication for this child and they stuck to psychostimulant medication. Frequently, doctors try to "medicate the problem away", label it safely as an ADHD disorder. No one communicates to find solutions for this young man. Solution steps for Larry and young persons with similar problems will include:

1. **An Individualized Educational Plan**: An IEP needs to be constructed for this child by state and federal law. HR 4303B guarantees disabled children with mental, emotional, and physical

disabilities and their parents that schools will provide special services to accommodate their needs. Whether a child is autistic, ADHD, developmentally delayed, or mood disordered, he or she deserves intervention at school. Therefore, an IEP team needs to set specific goals, objectives: (what will he do when faced with a stressor?), or (what will she do to increase her time on task with only one re-directive?) and ways to measure them for an impaired student.

2. **Hold IEP Team meetings to reach solutions**. The IEP team may include parents, a teacher, the school psychologist who conducts testing and classroom evaluations, a school counselor, district representative who supervises the provision of special education, the special education teacher, and the therapist or treating psychologist. This team needs to consult or work with the treating physician or child psychiatrist.

3. **Parents and the child keep a daily mood and sleep log** with a sleep diary and a short list of key events for the day that trigger stress or anxiety. It will be helpful for parents and the child to keep behavioral, mood, and sleep diaries on their son or daughter, along with a mood chart, a sleep log, a list of medications with dosages of medication taken each day. They write down any events that may trigger a mood, behavioral change or create anxiety or panic for their child.

<u>**Remember that many individuals confuse anxiety and mania.**</u> Anxiety is generally related to future or anticipated events, fear of making a mistake, or fear of heights, needles, animals, or fear of crowds and being examined or scrutinized by others.

<u>**Hypomanic mood is nervous or tense mood**</u>, a sensation of being pressured or pushed to do things quickly. Hypomania can include feelings of irritability, anger, and impulsively speaking one's mind or telling someone to back off.

Demitri Papolos, M.D. and Janice Papolos wrote the **Bipolar Child,** Papolos and Papolos (2002). In Chapter Five they provide very helpful charting ideas for charting changes in sleep, mood, anger, energy. I highly recommend that parents read this book including Chapter Five towards designing their own child's mood, sleep and energy charts. These authors write about sleep problems and how erratic sleep affects waking up, concentration, and changes in energy. These authors link sleep loss and mood changes.

Dr. Papolos cautions treatment providers in their use of antidepressant medication with bipolar youth (or Cyclothymic children and adolescents) as this medication can trigger mood switching. This psychologist recommends parents, and other adults working with these students, obtain and read a copy of this guide from their library or bookstore to get a thorough understanding of the treatment of mood disorders, related sleep disturbance, their treatment and management.

**Summary:**

Mood and sleep-charting information can be shared with the treatment team so that this team of providers will have data to assess the effect of medication. For any mood troubled student to do well, his treatment team (physician, nurse practitioner, or pediatrician and therapist) need to talk and dialogue with his IEP team at school and thereby, all may encourage positive directions. When everyone is aware of the student's mood, behavioral and health symptoms and mixed mood symptoms, specific guidelines and treatment plans can be planned to help such a moody child.

When the treatment team and the school IEP team having a comprehensive picture of all mood signs and symptoms, they provide this information to the treating psychiatrist. With this information this doctor may formulate an effective medical treatment plan. This treatment plan can help stabilize mood and improve sleep patterns for middle and high school students with Cyclothymic disorder or other mood disorders. Chapter 3 presents detailed examples of students with sleep problems and insomnia.

*Chapter 3*

# Susie Lacks Sleep

---

Cyclothymic children and teenagers struggle to sleep. They frequently are unable to go to sleep because their minds are too active or over-stimulated by television programs and computer games. Yet the average child with a calm mind can sleep. However, the Cyclothymic child is not average. He has a restless mind and energetic, restless mood and body. He finds himself wound up in the evenings and finds it hard to fall asleep.

Sleep problems include not being able to fall asleep for hours, waking at all hours, being unable to fall back asleep and difficulty waking in the morning. This erratic sleep is a "rough side and rough ride" of having Cyclothymic mood. This insomnia is a bio-genetic, biochemical problem that requires medical treatment with mood stabilization medication and help by healthy nutrition.

Frequently I ask parents and patients the question: "How many sleep disorders are there?" Ten? Twenty?" Most guess that there are 8 or 10. Sleep web sites and the National Sleep Foundation report there are 70 different sleep disorders. These sleep disorders are grouped in 3 categories:

- Lack of sleep (e.g., insomnia)
- Disturbed sleep (e.g., obstructive sleep apnea (OSA))
- Excessive sleep (e.g., narcolepsy).

In 1994 a University of Michigan Health System team followed and studied 257 preschool boys between the ages of 3 and 5, and their parents regarding difficulty sleeping. Ten years later Zucker found that these same children with poor sleep habits as preschoolers were "more than twice as likely to have substance abuse problems in adolescence." Dr. Robert Zucker stated that a biological factor that affects childhood sleep may increase the risk of substance abuse. He described it as a "shared neurobiological dysfunction whose details we don't yet know." (Zucker, et al., 1994, 2004)

Might it be a mood disorder, a Cyclothymic disorder, or hypomanic mood? More research needs to be done to research mood, sleep dysfunction in teenagers and its relationship to poor eating habits, substance abuse, marijuana use, or abuse of amphetamines and opioids. Some nighttime medications cause sleep problems.

**Case Example of a sleep disordered student**

Susie *, age 8, is an intelligent, precocious girl who liked to talk about 'a fun day with her aunt' and became animated when talking about a Halloween party with her cousins. Her grandmother brought her in for an evaluation because Susie had conflict with family members. She was aggressive and oppositional towards her mother. (This girl's name was changed to protect her family's privacy).

During the Clinical Interview this mental health provider wanted to get to the heart of the matter and asked Susie what she would like to change. She had her list ready in her mind and heart:

- "Want to change is that me and my (older) brother fight a lot."
- "Want to change that my big brother (age 12) does not pick on me."
- "I want to change that my mother talks a lot."
- "I want to change that my brother does not call me names."
- "I want to change that my brother does not make me angry."

Susie knows exactly what stresses her.

Susie's parents were administered a child behavior rating form (*CBCL Ages 4 – 18, 1991*) to complete and rate her behaviors. They reported that Susie often does not pay attention to details, doesn't seem to listen, can't follow directions and is easily distracted and forgetful. Parents found that Susie often fidgets, talks too much, argues, loses her temper, and acts defiantly. Her parents reported that she sleeps less than most kids, sulks a lot, threatens others and has a hot temper.

As is often the case, grandparents can be valuable source of clinical information on children. When parents are busy working and faced with challenges in providing for their children, grandparents, teachers, and caretakers provide valuable diagnostic information on behavior and mood. Susie's grandmother, Diane, is a good example. Susie often spent evenings or nights over at grandmother's home. Her grandmother reported that Susie sometimes bit her arms when she got mad, waited for her family to go to sleep, and then watched television for hours.

Grandmother Diane commented spontaneously that: "she has been awake two nights all night long.". This information about her 8-year-old granddaughter is a *valuable sign* pointing to a Cylothymic Disorder and hypomanic mood. Hypomanic mood is experienced when this young lady has a period or time of "high-strung activity and restless energy". With this mood she is unable to calm her mind or body, and she is too nervous to sleep in a restful and calm manner. With such a restless night of poor, meager sleep, it's not a surprise that the next day does not go well for Susie. Her grandmother reported that she had irritable, stubborn mood the next morning and "she refused to get her shoes on a couple of mornings." Diane observed that Susie lacks control of her verbal expression, her emotions, and she is impulsive.

**Family History of Mood, Sleep and Eating Disorders**

Interestingly, all female members in the family, grandmother, mother and daughters have mood disorders, mood swings, sleep problems and are obese. Bipolar spectrum disorders encourage a craving for carbohydrate foods and eating those foods with sugar added drinks or diet drinks may cause obesity. Chapter 7 describes healthier, alternative eating of (natural) fat and protein foods. Such eating practices leads to increased energy, higher metabolism and weight loss.

Suzie faces adversity at home and school, has peers and siblings tease her, battles fatigue and distractibility related to her lack of sleep. It is not surprising to see her have suicidal ideation at this age with her possible Cyclothymic disorder.

**Results of Psychological Testing with Susie:**

We administered the CAST story-telling test (Schneider, 1989) with Susie, and she made up stories for pictures of school scenes, peer situations, and family events. She showed an ability to problem solve in a positive manner and find solutions to end stories well for the participants. She expressed higher than average self-inadequacy, conflict with others, and negative emotions.

The Wechsler Individual Intelligence Scale, 3rd edition (WISC-III) was administered and Susie obtained Average Verbal and Performance IQ scores. In administering Wechsler IQ tests to children and adults with mood disorders, this clinician typically finds that they have a wide range of scaled scores. Nervous or depressed mood may deflate some of their scores, particularly scores on verbal items that require listening, concentration and no hands-on activity.

Frequently young people with insomnia, depressive episodes, and nervous mood have long range learning problems and lack confidence in testing. Most testing results with mood disordered students will show some low scores and impaired testing (score) results related to mood problems, distractibility and sleep loss. At the time of her evaluation, this psychologist diagnosed Susie with a Mood Disorder, NOS and a Circadian Rhythm Sleep Disorder. Today this psychologist would diagnose her as having a Cyclothymic Disorder with related insomnia or sleep disturbance.

**Medical and School Interventions to Help Her Succeed**

*Recommendations* to Susie's parents were as follows:

1. Parents were encouraged to consult their pediatrician with her psychological evaluation and plan medical evaluation and treatment

of her Cyclothymic Disorder. This provider recommended that her physician refer her to a child psychiatrist to evaluate and treat her *Cycling* mood disorder and sleep disturbance.

2. Parents are encouraged to work with the IEP intervention team at school to construct an effective individual educational plan, and to work with the school psychologist, the special education representative, her school teachers and principal to ensure she receives supportive care and interventions at school.

3. Parents were encouraged to pair Susie with a big sister through a social service agency and have her participate in Girl Scouts or a church group to develop social skills and increase her self-confidence.

Before we present a second example, let's examine a study by Van Meter A. et al., (2011) with an outpatient clinical sample of 827 youth (ages 5 to 17). These researchers found that the 52 Cyclothymic youth differed from behavior disordered youth: "on irritability, sleep disturbance, age of symptom onset, comorbid diagnosis, and family history." (Van Meter, et al., (2011): 55-63.)

The example of Susie is a good illustration of the results found by Van Meter, et al., 2011. She has sleep disturbance, has a family history of bipolar disorder, has irritability, a combative, angry temperament, and mood changes as do family members.

**A Teenager with sleep disturbance:**

My second example of insomnia and sleep disturbance is a teenage boy named Bryan, age 16. He attended an area high school and came with his mother for psychological evaluation and testing. His mother was particularly concerned with his poor academic performance, his inability to keep up with schoolwork, and that he only completed half of his schoolwork.

Bryan's mother reported that his school problems began in the fourth grade. He had a lack of interest and participation in school, had periods of depression and sleep problems. She reported: "Bryan can't sleep at night, so he can't get up to go to school." In describing his trouble sleeping she added:

> "He goes to bed, but can't sleep. By the time he goes to sleep, he can't get up in the a.m." She reported that "he has truancy problems and is late to school." "Bryan is a precocious teenager and has wide interests including fishing, riding his bicycle and his motorcycle. Compared to others his age he spends more than average time with his hobbies of cars, motorcycle, and average time with crafts and models." His mother listed his job interests as mechanic, electronic work, and science.

## Psychological Testing Results for Bryan:

Parents, school districts, doctors, and mental health practitioners including psychologists often request cognitive and intellectual functioning assessment to determine the teenager's abilities, strengths and weaknesses. Dr. Paulus administered the WISC-III with Bryan to determine how his mental health problems and possible ADHD impacted his WISC-III scores and performance.

Bryan obtained average scaled scores of 10 on the Verbal tests of Information, Similarities, (a verbal reasoning task), and Comprehension. He scored poorly on the Verbal tests of Arithmetic (scaled score of 3), and Digit Span (score of 5), tests that reflect his concentration/ distractibility problem. His low score on these two tasks, suggests that Bryan has difficulty focusing on one thing at a time. He obtained a low Average Verbal IQ score, and a low Average Performance IQ score.

## A Calming Medication Increased His Ability to Focus

Bryan had just begun taking Divalproex sodium (Depakote), 750 mg. daily, a low dose of an anticonvulsant, mood stabilization medication.

Usually divided, mild doses of this medication is recommended with liver function tests and blood labs. He reported that he felt tired, yet he was motivated during this testing.

He was sufficiently focused that he began to correct his errors on the Block Design test. As his racing, distractible mind slowed to a reasonable speed, he was able to make positive self-instructions and tell himself such things as: "I'm thinking of something else" and "I got sidetracked here." He went back to check the design and changed the orientation of blocks to make an accurate design. With a more complex design, Bryan struggled and lost track of some detail of the design. He proceeded slowly and corrected and corrected again to complete his design. He completed the last complex design in rapid fashion. It was amazing to see how this young man improved his concentration, increased his motivation and persistence, and increased his ability to refocus.

Bryan's parents completed the Conners' Rating Scales and marked the following items as true for him: Picks at things (ie., nails, fingers), has problems with making or keeping friends, wanting to run things, having difficulty in learning, and being fearful of new people or places/ going to school. They saw him as restless and always up and on- the-go, shy, failing to finish things, having distractibility, disliking rules or restrictions, and having sleep problems.

These behavioral signs typify a teenager with a Cyclothymic Disorder. His distractibility index score on the WISC-III may be another sign that he has excitable mood with racing thoughts reflecting a Cyclothymic Disorder with hypomanic mood episodes.

On a depression inventory Bryan marked that he "does not want to be with people at all". He also marked that he has to push himself to do school work, that he is tired many days, and that he has trouble sleeping every night. He commented about sleep: "I lay there and can't fall asleep". "I lay there and I toss and turn." This restless sleep behavior suggests the presence of hypomanic mood.

**Treatment Plan for Bryan included:**

1.  Encourage Bryan to follow up with his physician and treating psychiatrist and share his sleep diary or sleep log. On the NIMH mood chart Bryan can chart and list his sleep hours for the night before and graph his mood changes. Five and a half hours are rounded up to six hours of sleep. Parents may want to share and discuss research with their physicians: such as Jacobsen FM. etal. (1993) regarding the use *"Low dose valproate"* (Depakote) as a treatment for cyclothymia, mild rapid cycling disorders. This medication was currently beginning to help this student.

2.  Have Bryan keep a sleep diary. He can write every evening or two and describe how he slept the night before. Encourage him to write in his sleep diary details such as: how long it took to go to sleep, how many times he woke up, did he toss and turn and kick his sheets around? How did he feel the next morning (tired? rested? little rested with low or average energy?). Then he will be able to share his weekly sleep diary with his treating psychiatrist. Together his family and his psychiatrist can monitor the effectiveness of his medication in encouraging a restful sleep pattern.

3.  He and one of his parents can discuss with his prescribing physician what positive changes they observed with his mood, motivation, his ability to focus and to correct his schoolwork. They need to assess to what extent his medication is helping improve his mood, his sleep, and his relationship with others at home and at school.

4.  Mood disordered young people need to be engaged in healthy, sociable activities to increase their motivation and improve their mood, to discharge extra (hypomanic) energy and to channel their natural energy toward helping others. By getting involved in church groups, school activities, scouts, or volunteer activities, these young people will experience how others appreciate them and want to be with them.

Such experiences build character, confidence, friendships, and social competence needed for a career or for joining the Armed Services. Young people may become motivated for working with such groups as the Peace Corps or conservation organizations like the Nature Conservancy or the Sierra Club to preserve natural habitats for animals and to save endangered animal species.

5.  Encourage these restless young people to wind down two hours before bedtime with quiet hands-on activities (drawing, puzzles, playing a chess game, othello). During school nights this psychologist counsels parents to have their children put away all cell phones and turn off all tv's and screen electronics to reduce stimulation of their children's minds and slow brain activity. These items need to be put aside an hour before bedtime and no later than 9 p.m.

    *Quiet, calming activity* needs to be encouraged before going to sleep, such as reading a story book, a novel, or drawing and doodling. Consider practice of spelling, and have your child or teen learn new vocabulary words from a dictionary, an encyclopedia, a Bible, or other religious text. They can try out their new vocabulary word by writing a short sentence using it. The reward is better grades.

6.  Sit down with your son or daughter and think of a goal for the school year. Perhaps have them learn to write a short book or some poetry. Encourage your son or daughter to draw animals or flowers and learn to sketch faces or buildings. These constructive activities encourage competence and self-confidence, teach children to master frustration, and redirect them from negative, self-defeating thinking. Such activities encourage peaceful, hopeful meditation that fosters sleep.

**Summary:**

Sleep disorders are a common problem for Cyclothymic children and teenagers. This cycling mood disorder encourages energy changes, changes of mood, restless mind with racing thoughts and frequent waking. A child with Cyclothymic disorder has erratic, variable sleep patterns and difficulty going to sleep because hypomanic mood often kicks in during the evening. Your child or teen's mind and body will become active at just the 'wrong time'.

Your teen or child doesn't kick into high gear intentionally. He will gravitate towards more stimulating activities, such as video games and watching tv and computer videos. Then it becomes difficult to calm your child for bedtime and sleep. Do stop all video activities that stimulate the brain, two hours before bedtime. Proceed with reading, writing, drawing activities before bedtime to calm your student's mind and body. With a good medical and behavioral treatment plan, you, the parent with your treatment team can direct your child to better sleep.

It may take a trial of the right 'sleep medication' (preferably not a brain activating antidepressant medication), beginning calm evening activities and stopping the consumption of carbohydrate and sugar foods 3 hours before bedtime to see improved sleep patterns. A tablespoon of virgin coconut oil added to salads, corn tortillas with protein, or a tuna sandwich, may aid sleep. Dr. Bruce Fife explains the benefit of this health food in Chapter 7.

### Resources: For Information in Evaluating Treating Sleep Problems

National Sleep Foundation 1522 K Street, NW, Suite 500 Washington, DC 20005

Papolos, D. and Papolos, J. (2002) **The Bipolar Child.** New York: Broadway Books.

Papolos, D. and Papolos, J. (1997) **Overcoming Depression**. New York: Broadway Books

Sleep Home Pages www.sleephomepages.org

Youth Info http://youth.hhs.gov

**Psychiatric Annals :** The Journal of Continuing Psychiatric Education, July 1987. Volume 17, Number 7 includes: **Sleep Disorders**, Leo Madow, M.D.: Evaluation and Treatment of Insomnia; Sleepwalking, Night Terrors, and Nightmares.

# Chapter 4

# Key Signs and Symptoms

---

**Introduction:**

It is helpful to know key signs and symptoms of Cyclothymic Disorder because:

- You can identify students with this mood change disorder more quickly. Parents and teachers may intervene effectively to help them be successful in school.
- Parents and concerned school staff may help direct mental health and medical treatment to save families and students considerable time in resolving behavioral and educational problems.
- Conflict, aggressive behavior, violence, self-destructive behavior, or suicide may be prevented.
- Cyclothymic students may not be diagnosed as ADHD, Disruptive behavior disorder or Oppositional Disordered students.

Cyclothymic disorders have key symptoms and signs that are helpful to know in quickly identifying children, adolescents, and students with this disorder. More efficient identification of these children leads to more rapid intervention. It may save months of time in treatment! More efficient diagnosis and identification can timely point out children at risk for suicide and violence. The next paragraph describes how this mood disorder differs from more chronic, severe forms of depression and manic-depressive illness.

Students may be diagnosed with Cyclothymic disorder when significant mood changes from depression to hypomania are present for a year or two. Moods can change from moderately irritable, restless, energetic mood with restless, impulsive behavior when the student is *hypomanic* to being *depressed.* The depressed student may be sad, whiny, withdrawn, and avoids interacting with others and avoids activities of interest.

Akiskal and Malya, 1987 found Cyclothymia was present in 5% of a 102 patient sample in a community mental health center sample and that bipolar spectrum conditions were as common as unipolar mood diagnosed patients. Akiskal et al., 2000 stated that "hypomania" is critical in the definition of cyclothymic disorder.

Studies reviewed on cyclothymia and hypomania were "unanimous in validating a duration of hypomania shorter than 4 days." (H.S. Akiskal et al, 2000): S11. Angst (1998) listed the following as most common signs of *hypomania* in a community study in the following table.

## Table 6

Less sleep
More energy, strength
More self-confidence
Increased activities (including working more)
Enjoying work more than usual
More social activities (ie., telephone calls, visiting other people)
Spending too much money
More plans and ideas
Less shy, less inhibited
More talkative than usual
Increased sex drive
Increased consumption: coffee, cigarettes, alcohol,
Overly optimistic/euphoric
Increased laughter (making jokes, puns)
Thinking fast, sudden ideas.

**Cyclothymic Disorder**

Children may be diagnosed with Cyclothymic Disorder when mood changes are present over a period of a year; and during this time the child or teenager is not without these symptoms for more than two months at a time.

Dr. Hagop Askikal, a psychiatrist who has devoted his life to the study of mood and personality disorders, has studied this mood disorder for over twenty-five years. He observed that individuals with cyclothymic disorder with their changes in temperament are *often mistaken* to be personality or character disorders. Children, teens, and adults with this mood disorder are known for their intense and frequent mood changes, daily or weekly highs and lows, and losses of judgment that accompany these mood changes.

Cyclothymic disorder is not diagnosed when it is due to a medical condition, effects of substance abuse, or mood symptoms due to a more severe mood disorder or mental health disorder.

**Key Signs and Symptoms**

Cyclothymic children can present with a mixture of symptoms that may look like Attention deficit/hyperactivity disorder, Conduct disorder and/or an Oppositional Defiant disorder. These children and teens can present with:

- hyperactive behavior and energetic mood
- anger outbursts and irritability
- concentration problems and distractibility
- a tendency to be talkative and disruptive in the classroom.
- enjoyment of being the center of attention when they are in an upbeat, expansive mood
- being painfully shy, withdrawn, and depressed.
- being restless and fidgety, and unable to sit still
- being impulsive in behavior and speech
- Some Cyclothymic mood swing youth lack internal controls and may destroy things at home and at school. They may get into fights when they believe they are being treated unfairly. These children and teenagers may be aggressive at times.

**Key signs and symptoms of cyclothymic disorder may include:**

1.  sleep disturbance including difficulty getting to sleep and waking frequently during the night, or having acute sleep deprivation
2.  frequent and sometimes rapid mood changes
3.  charged-up, hyperactive, or energetic mood and behavior
4.  problems with attention, concentration, or listening to others
5.  periods of depressed mood that may be moderately severe
6.  destructive or aggressive behavior or being verbally aggressive
7.  learning problems
8.  oppositional behavior and conduct problems

Askikal et al., 1998 cited the <u>following criteria</u> for the cyclothymic (young adult): Biphasic mood swings--abrupt shifts from one phase (depressive or hypomanic) to the other, each phase lasting for a few days. They stated that at least four of the following mood shifts will be present for the young person to constitute the habitual long-term baseline of the subject:

- lethargy alternating with *upbeat mood/ restless, energetic mood.*
- shaky self-esteem alternating between *low self-confidence and overconfidence*
- decreased verbal output alternating with *talkativeness*
- mental confusion alternating with *sharpened and creative thinking*
- unexplained tearfulness alternating with *excessive punning and jocularity*
- introverted self-absorption alternating with *uninhibited people-seeking.*

**Activity level:**

Children or teenagers with cyclothymic disorder will vary in activity level depending on mood state. When in a hyperthymic, upbeat mood, they may be rather active and socially engaged during the school day, at home, at church, or when involved with groups. They will thrive in soccer, an active sport.

When a teenager shifts into hypomanic mood, he becomes very talkative, over-involved and sometimes intrusive or bossy. During depressed mood, these same young persons will withdraw, avoid others, and lose confidence in social, academic, and other activities. School performance can drop off considerably and often these children and teenagers 'forget their homework'.

## Cognition:

Mood disorders have a subtle effect on learning, IQ and achievement, and the Variables of Attention (TOVA) computer test. One young man (age 6) in a rather hyperthymic mood continually drummed his fingers on the desk and swiveled back and forth in his chair during TOVA(R) testing. He obtained a significant number of Errors of 'Commission' (impulsivity) as he pushed the micro-switch too quickly at the wrong time.

Similar testing results occurred with the newer CPT-II computer test for assessing inattention, impulsivity, and vigilance. Adults and children in depressed states may become increasingly fatigued or sleepy and make more errors as this ADHD computer test continues to later phases. Alhola and Polo-Kantola observed that decrease in attention and working memory due to (SD) sleep deprivation is well established, along with impaired vigilance with the psychomotor vigilance test (PVT). (Alhola and Polo-Kantola, 2007): 555-556.

Cyclothymic teenagers have increased problems with language, with listening to passages read and understanding appropriate meanings. Errors are frequent with writing or spelling. Many of these teenagers and pre-teens may be diagnosed as 'learning disabled' or 'special education' students. Often they may need these 'diagnoses' to be eligible for tutoring and extra accommodations.

Due to their excitable, hypomanic, and nervous mood, these teenagers face a challenge with the Wechsler Intelligence Scale for Children (WISC-IV). Their excitable mood encourages them to rush and work impulsively with the Block Design test (and other verbal and non-verbal tests). Manic-depressive teenagers, whether in high school or college level, will race past possible solutions and move their blocks so rapidly that they *skip past solutions* when they are right in front of them. They quickly move on to a different design or solution attempt. I often comment to them: "You had the solution and you whipped past it in part of a second!"

Likewise, on verbal tests of the WISC-IV, the examiner needs to give these sometimes depressed, less confident students a second cue. For example: "I believe you may have a better answer for how these 2 words are alike. Take a little more time to think and see what you come up with." When in a depressed state, students need a little more encouragement. When in a hyperthymic or hypomanic mood, these students need to be encouraged to take their time and not settle for one rapid, impulsive answer. When so encouraged, these students often come up with a better answer.

## Energy:

The hyperthymic and hypomanic child has considerable energy and may easily outlast her (or his) peers with day or night-time activities. They may be very enthusiastic and charged-up and enjoy after school sports, theatre, and other activities. Parents find them difficult to corral at night and to discourage them from playing video or computer games. By staying up late nights and losing sleep and energy, by early morning, these students have problems with lack of energy, motivation, and being disorganized when they need to quickly get up and go to school.

When the Cyclothymic child has a depressive episode, he lacks motivation, and often refuses to do schoolwork. There is little confidence or energy for schoolwork or projects. They prefer to be left alone and to stay in their rooms. When depressed, they become listless, lethargic, and are not able to move or be moved. Chores become difficult.

## Mood:

The hyperthymic child is energetic, outgoing, sociable, motivated, and sometimes irritable. Hypomanic mood may include three or more of the following for 2 or more days: cheerfulness, joking behavior, heightened sexual drive and behavior, talkativeness, overconfidence, and over-optimism, and hyposomnia (typically sleeping 5 or 6 hours). These students may show gregariousness or people-seeking behavior and over-involvement in new projects (Askikal, et al., 2005, 1979; Hantouche et al., 2003).

When hypomanic mood persists, sleep deprivation may become a serious problem as attention, vigilance decreases, mistakes and accidents can occur. These students can make poor judgments, and become increasingly irritable and argumentative.

The depressed Cyclothymic teenager or child may have periods of sad mood, hypersomnia, withdrawn behavior, decreased energy. They may have low self-confidence, periodic suicidal thinking, social anxiety, or panic attacks. Motivation for tasks at home and school decrease. For parents and teachers, these students are hard to budge or encouraged towards action. Adults and mentors in their lives will need to find new, novel ways of motivating these students to change their behavior, to work in treatment, and to work well in the school setting with the intervention team.

**Sleep:**

Sleep is a particular problem for children and adolescents with Cyclothymic disorder and this mood disorder effects both the duration and the quality of sleep.

**Bad results from this mood disorder include:**

1. Disruption of sleep and sleep patterns. Sleeping only 4 or 5 hours.
2. Difficulty going to sleep, and frequent waking are typical.
3. Excessive thinking through the night, revaluations of the day gone by, and what could have been gone better.
4. Presence of *racing thoughts related to hypomania*. This restless mental state keeps these students awake for hours and keeps them tossing and turning. Sleep deprivation may lead to daytime sleepiness.
5. The Cyclothymic student wakes up tired and irritable.

When the teenager doesn't sleep well, all areas and aspects of school performance are negatively affected. Steenari et al., (2003) found that sleep quality and quantity affect performance of working memory tasks in school age children (6 to 13). They concluded: "In children with learning difficulties the possibility of underlying sleep problems should be evaluated." (p.85.). See Figure 5

Parents frequently tell me that these young people are hard to get up in the mornings and they often get ready at the last minute. Forgetting to take things to school and 'forgetting' at home and at school is not uncommon for these sleep-deprived Cyclothymic students.

### Working Memory and Sleep in 6 to 13 Year-old School Children

- **This study has 68 children from Finland who attended regular classes**
- **Sleep quality and quantity was assessed by wrist worn actigraphs (Steenari et al.,)**
- **Working memory tasks consisted of audio and visuospatial n-back tasks with three different load levels.**
- **Children with poor sleep quality made more mistakes in the more demanding tasks (2 back-tasks).**
- **Poorer sleep quality was associated with a reduced ability to remember both auditory and visual stimuli; yet auditory tasks proved to be more difficult to remember.**

Figure 5: Steenari et al., 2003

It is typical for cyclothymic children, students to get appreciably less sleep than their peers during the night and the quality of their sleep will be poor. They may toss and turn most of the night or get up repeatedly to check on things. During the day they are tired, less focused, more irritable, and their ability to be attentive and to learn is impaired. During the evening they may nap and have little motivation to do schoolwork. Parents often comment how 'difficult it is to get them to do their homework'.

A mother and her 12-year-old student came to see me to obtain help for school. They described his problems as social anxiety and lack of motivation to do schoolwork. He initially presented as being very shy and was prescribed an antidepressant to treat his social anxiety and mild depressed mood. His mother reported that he was very hyper today, and that the boy demonstrated that by talking up a storm and making funny noises. She stated: "He couldn't sit still" since starting this medication. We saw him as being "restless in his behavior". His mother stated that "lately he has been having trouble sleeping" and that his sleeping is getting worse.

I realized this boy had a mood swing, engineered by his doctor prescribing an antidepressant medication. His doctor had not diagnosed a possible mood spectrum disorder like Cyclothymic Disorder. My psychological evaluation included recommendations to his pediatrician to try a new direction with psychopharmacology to help this boy improve his sleep.

In Chapter 6 we will look in detail at various mood disorders including antidepressant induced Hypomanic mood. Dr. Ronald Fieve, 1989 described how such a serotonin syndrome is created.

Chapter 5 goes into detail on how Cyclothymic Disorder encourages disruptive behavior and changing moods at school and discourages learning and achievement of good grades. We will examine how this mood disorder affects teenagers in school, home, and social settings.

**Summary**

Cyclothymic Disorder is a mood disorder that encourages or causes problems with:

1. Rapid mood swings from hypomanic, energetic, or restless mood and behavior to avoidant, quiet, withdrawn behavior and depressed mood
2. Disrupted sleep including difficulty going to sleep, frequent waking during the night, and difficulty waking up in the morning. Acute

sleep deprivation is possible and will have a negative effect on school performance including impaired attention and vigilance.

3. Disruptive, sometimes angry, aggressive behavior.
4. Learning problems due to distractibility, impaired vigilance, decreased working memory, racing thoughts, and rushing through tasks with a lack of patience.
5. The student having a tendency toward impulsive, risk-taking behavior which results in injury, car accidents, alcohol and drug use, early sexual behavior, and harm towards self or others.

Chapters 5 through 10 go into greater detail on these topics.

*Chapter 5*

# Cyclothymic Disorder in the School Setting

---

## Introduction

Children and students with cyclothymic disorder show impulsive behavior, do things quickly without thinking, and rush through tasks. Their minds tell them: 'Go faster, faster!' Sudden changes in mood, such as anger or being sullen and impatient, are common in these children. They may quickly get a negative thought or attitude towards a learning task. As a result, their efforts to learn and to complete a task go downhill quickly.

School becomes increasingly frustrating as they may have difficulty concentrating on the details of such tasks as spelling, writing, and remembering assignments. Working in a calm, slow, patient manner on mundane work like practicing spelling words, writing sentences and paragraphs for short essays, may be difficult for them.

### Case Example: Frustrated Martin

Seven-year-old Martin looked considerably smaller than others his age. He and his family entered my office in a flourish and Martin made a beeline from the waiting room to the clinician's office requesting to be first to be seen. When he was first seen, his grandmother reported that he frequently got into fights. She also reported restless behavior, low frustration tolerance, and sloppy eating habits. He had problems with cursing, lying, changing appetite and aggressive behavior. Both his mother and his teacher completed the Achenbach Child Behavior Checklist (CBCL 4-18, 1991).

His teacher reported that Martin's language and reading level were well below grade level, and his math performance was below grade level. His parents are bright individuals and his mother works as a lawyer, yet Martin receives tutoring to improve his language skills. His teacher expressed concern about his refusal to do what is expected of him which led to confrontations and to encouraging negative behavior in peers.

## He showed Cyclothymic disorder behavior and signs:

His 2nd grade teacher listed the following problems: making odd noises in class, arguing a great deal, failing to finish things, being defiant and talking back, and being restless. She saw him fidgeting, being cruel and bullying others. She reported the following frequent behaviors: demanding attention, disturbing other students, cheating, and biting and chewing his fingernails. He had problems with being overweight, physically attacking others and picking his skin. Martin preferred being with older students.

His teacher reported that Martin often had messy work and behaved irresponsibly. She saw that he had explosive and unpredictable behavior, was inattentive and distractible, became irritable, and had sudden changes in *mood or feelings.* He had a hot temper while making threats towards others. He disliked school, underachieved, and sulked a lot. These behaviors and mood changes suggested a Cyclothymic disorder with a possible sleep disorder. Doctors and mental health providers may not examine sleep disorders. As a result, students like Martin do not receive comprehensive treatment.

## Martin Needed treatment

Martin and his mother were referred to a treating child psychiatrist who could further evaluate and treat his mood disorder and evaluate possible sleep disturbance. His moodiness, nervous behavior, and unpredictable and aggressive behavior suggested a Cyclothymic Disorder. Martin's mother signed a record release authorization and his psychological evaluation report was faxed to his treating physician.

Social anxiety is frequently related to Cyclothymic disorder and other bipolar spectrum disorders. Young persons may easily be embarrassed or feel awkward in social situations. They often feel that others are judging or scrutinizing them to find weaknesses and faults. Substance abuse problems are common and are a way for Cyclothymic teenagers and pre-teens to cope with the social anxiety, general anxiety, depression, mood changes.

## How Does Cyclothymic Disorder Affect Children and Teenagers?

### Sleep problems.

Sleep problems are common and may include difficulty falling asleep, being fearful of the dark, restless sleep and sleep deprivation. Waking up easily due to 'light sleep', or hearing sounds/ noises is a common occurrence. One 6 -year-old student who was talkative, excited, hypomanic during interviews commented: "My blanket helps me fall asleep." Therapy for this boy involved individual and family therapy to help him find ways to feel more secure at night. He, his family and this therapist brainstormed several ideas that the family could do to make his room feel safe for him.

Children with mood disorders reported fears of robbers breaking in at night, of ghosts representing recently deceased family walking near their bedrooms. Or they imagine other dangerous persons breaking in to harm their family. These children have vivid imaginations and active minds during the night. They often work hard to stay up as late as possible to avoid the imagined impending threat or danger.

It is typical for Cyclothymic mood disordered students to get appreciably less sleep than their peers during the night and the quality of their sleep is inferior. They may toss and turn most of the night and kick their sheets or stuffed animals off the bed. During the day they are tired, less attentive, and more irritable. They find it difficult to concentrate or be vigilant with tasks. During the evening they may nap and have little motivation to do schoolwork.

## Mood Disorders and Loss of Control of Behavior

When sleep is disturbed or inferior, these students may have irritable mood, be short-tempered or angry and easily frustrated, and lack motivation to achieve and do schoolwork. When they come home from school, they prefer to nap rather than do their schoolwork. Parents often comment how 'difficult it is to get her to do her work' or "how long she takes to do a brief assignment; sometimes sitting there for hours."

During May 2002 a local newspaper ran a story titled: *"4 student threats, 4 different responses."* A sixth grader had written out a "hit list" of several people, real and made-up. He was suspended for 10 days. The same week in April, four sixth graders at the same school wrote down the names of a dozen people they didn't like. All four were expelled for the rest of the school year.

Also last month, another suburban fifth- grader wrote down the names of six students he wanted to shoot. He was assigned to a counseling program that will keep him out of school for the rest of the year. The newspaper story described a local sixth grade girl who named seven students and two teachers on a list that she titled: "People I want to die or kill." This girl was charged with a delinquency count of inducing panic.

### *My question:*

Do any of these consequences help these students? Do these interventions and punishments solve the problem and show these students how to behave and express themselves properly in the future? No, they are incomplete.

These consequences are *overly simple* solutions and responses to maladaptive, immature behavior by emotionally disturbed students. These students may suffer with mood and sleep disorders. They may have Cyclothymic disorders with mixed mood states and become agitated easily. To really help these children the school, community and court system need to do the following:

1. Provide and administer psychological testing of these young people. Such testing would include the Millon Pre-Adolescent Clinical Inventory (M-PACI) (for ages 9 to 12) to assess emotional and psychological functioning and what coping skills are present.

2. Administer sleep, mood, anxiety inventories and have parents and teachers complete behavior inventories / checklists with these students. There is a need to assess anxiety, stress, sleep and mood patterns. This data can be provided to a treatment team.

3. Have a psychologist interview these children, parents and teachers separately to get an understanding of what is going on emotionally with each student and within the family and school setting. We need to know the internal and external stressors these students experience.

4. Refer these students to a pediatrician and a child psychiatrist with a report from the psychologist, school psychologist or court social worker. Mood and sleep inventory results and ratings of behavior checklists need to be shared with the treating psychiatrist. Sleep deprived, stressed, and mood disordered children feel very vulnerable and will lash out or threaten others to defend themselves. Sleep deprivation and certain mood disorders will encourage paranoid thinking, paranoid behavior, and related aggressive behavior. (Meloy, 1989)

5. All these students need IEP's in the school setting. There needs to be coordination and communication among parents, teachers, medical providers, and these students to prevent harm to others and towards themselves. It is preferable that parents and these emotional/ mood disturbed students work with a mental health court to guide and supervise their treatment and behavior.

## Learning Problems

The Cyclothymic student often has learning problems that may begin during the elementary school years. Due to a 'restless', distractible mind, this student often has difficulty with a variety of subjects. A teacher recently commented regarding her eight-year-old student: "His weakness is language, particularly written language. It takes him too long to write." Teachers report that these children tend to rush through their work or refuse to do it for periods of time (until they are again in the mood). Impulsive behavior is frequent with these children.

When they play games, they make their moves rapidly. They lack patience for games with too much reading, and they quickly lose interest and request another activity. An energetic, impulsive child often may do things quickly without thinking. They begin to make mistakes on the schoolwork, and their motivation to complete work decreases. They may stop doing their assignments.

## Peer and Friendship Problems

Sometimes hasty words cause conflict with peers and friendships may become strained or broken. The changes in mood and temperament and rapid shifts in behavior may encourage peers to wonder about their relations with these young people. "Should we stay friends?" After a time the circle of friends grows smaller.

The Cyclothymic student shows a variety of mood and behavior symptoms. Mood swings are characteristic and these teenagers may show sad mood and constricted affect, or have restless, nervous mood and behavior. Thinking may be marked by distrust and wariness of others.

These mood swing teenagers often blame others for their problems, and see others as trying to find fault with them. Suicidal ideation may occur. When such nervous and depressive mood symptoms persist or cause serious impairment, a Cyclothymic disorder or bipolar disorder needs to be evaluated. Medical treatment needs to begin immediately.

The Cyclothymic teen has a strong desire to fit in with their peer group, and sometimes will go to great lengths to be part of a group. Substance use and marijuana abuse may be part of this teenager's effort to manage their mood swings, nervousness, anxiety, tension. They have a strong desire to feel an important part of their peer group.

**Family**

Family life is strongly impacted by the presence of a mood disorder in one or more family members. Family arguments, ignoring rules, challenging family rules and temper tantrums may occur. Kicking walls, kicking, or hitting family members, yelling, and other aggressive behavior may be part of family life. These mood related behaviors increase stress for individuals within the family. Cyclothymic and bipolar students find it difficult to listen, to follow rules, and they often believe they can set their own course.

**School adjustment:**

The Cyclothymic student often has considerable problems adjusting to the school setting. Absences are common and often related to social anxiety and lack of motivation. Dropping out of school is frequent along with getting involved with the wrong crowd. These adolescents may lack the patience, concentration, and the motivation achieve. Teachers' comments, encouragement, and corrections are often seen as attacks or insults. "I'm not stupid!"; or "I'd wish they'd get off my back." are frequently heard comments these young people make about their interactions with their teachers.

These mood cycling students often dislike school because they can't relax and achieve like their peers. One teenager remarked that she was so irritated by her teacher she wanted to throw him out of the window. After she had been treated with a mood stabilization medication (an anticonvulsant medicine) for several weeks, she felt considerably calmer and more at ease in the school setting. Her attitude and feelings towards her teacher became more positive. "He doesn't bother me anymore," she commented.

**What causes cyclothymic disorder?**

Key words in answering this question include GABA, Glutamate, balance, excitability, and mood stabilization.

Some twenty years ago I attended an excellent seminar with a psycho-pharmacologist from North Carolina who treated children, teenagers, and adults for depression, bipolar mood disorders, and anxiety. He made on comment that stuck with me for years: "Did you know that the best anxiety medication is anticonvulsant medication." "It works to restore the GABA – Glutamate balance in the brain. Glutamate encourages excitability, anxiety, nervousness. GABA is a neurochemical that encourages calming of the brain."

Cyclothymic disorder is believed to be caused by an imbalance in brain chemistry when certain neuro-chemicals such as serotonin, norepinephrine, dopamine, glutamate and GABA have shifts in their availability to the brain cells and to brain structures like the Amygdala and the Hippocampus. Too much stress and stimulation, too little restful sleep, lack of healthy fat in the diet, too much sugar, carbohydrate, or gluten consumed, can overwhelm these emotional centers of the brain.

Like other medical conditions such as diabetes, heart disease, attention deficit disorder, there is a strong family genetic history and susceptibility linked to this illness. When there is a family history of depression or manic depression, there is a likelihood the child or teenager will have Cyclothymic mood disorder with depressive episodes.

Cyclothymic students and bipolar adults have frequently commented to me on "feeling overwhelmed" at school in a noisy class or in a crowded work environment, like a fast food restaurant. "I had to get out and leave, or I would have had a panic attack", patients told me. There was too much stimulation, talking, noise exciting their nervous system.

When these restless students with sleep deprivation are over stimulated and unable to manage or modulate their arousal systems, they become very distracted, anxious, and annoyed. Such a mood disordered, mood swing student who is overanxious or nervous is at a disadvantage in testing, in learning, and in managing a work environment.

For this reason, this psychologist included IEP recommendations to the university disability office and to public schools. I suggested that the Cyclothymic student needs a quiet, non-distracting testing room provided; and thereby they may be able to think clearly and in a calm manner and arrive at test answers as less emotional peers do. For cyclothymic students we need to reduce stimulation in the room to prevent anxiety and nervous mood. We need to make testing fair and equitable for these mood swing students.

## CYCLOTHYMIC DISORDER IN TEENAGERS

Teenagers have a host of life demands facing them at this stage. They face the challenge of managing a continual twisting- and-turning array of feelings and moods. Teenagers with Cyclothymic disorder who have mood episodes have a more challenging time than their peers in coping with life's demands. Teens may experience subtle mood changes to more obvious mood swings, and these young persons may turn to different 'safe havens' at stressful times.

Often students turn to drugs and alcohol to help them manage the varying emotions associated with their mood disorder. One 14-year-old female teenager commented: "I've used all kinds of drugs. I preferred weed. It calmed me. I was more mellow. No one irritated me."

Family life is full of wrangles, frustrations, and arguments for these teenagers. Often their bright, creative, strong-willed, assertive, temperamental, and argumentative natures and their 'know-it-all' attitudes will clash with their parent's wishes. Family conflict and stress frequently is a reason these young persons are brought in for counseling.

Cyclothymic students have a low tolerance for the school setting. Restlessness, low frustration tolerance, impatience, difficulty concentrating are some of the factors which make school difficult and frequently intolerable for them. Arguments with teachers, forgetting homework, suspensions and expulsions, and absences are frequent events for these students.

### Case Example of A Depressed, Moody, Unmotivated Teenager

Sally's parents referred this 14-year-old student for psychological treatment and testing. She lacked motivation for school, seemed depressed, and often argued with her parents. Sally had recently been sexually active, and this behavior concerned her parents. Promiscuity and increased sexual desire is a common sign of hypomanic mood. She used drugs and reported that marijuana helped calm her and her restless mood.

Upon inquiry about her traits and mood as a child, her mother reported that she was always an angry child, and that she has been even more irritable, and angry lately. She has had noticeable mood symptoms for two years; and she had thoughts of suicide by age 12. Sally had increasing frustration and problems with school. She had difficulty doing her schoolwork at home and at school and her grades were dropping. Concentration, lack of motivation, and depression were problems and suicidal thoughts were present.

Structured, diagnostic interviews with Sally and her parents along with child behavior checklist results indicated a Cyclothymic disorder. Sally showed increasingly temperamental, irritable mood. Her parents worried that she would have similar problems to last year's depressive episode. Sally reported chronic sleep problems, restlessness, racing thoughts, and excessive worrying.

She and her parents were referred to a psychiatrist for treatment. Initially, she was treated with antidepressants with little result. Her sleep problems and depression continued. Her psychiatrist initiated a dosage of an anticonvulsant medication, Depakote 250 mg, bid., and increased this dosage gradually. This medication is an anticonvulsant, GABA medication that frequently calms mood and racing thoughts. Sally's mood *improved considerably*, her depression disappeared, sleep patterns normalized, and her concentration improved along with her school grades. Her diagnosis was accurate.

Follow-up visits with her psychologist for individual and family therapy, and her psychiatrist for medication were continued as part of her needed ongoing treatment.

## Similar Research Results

Similar results were shared by Verhoeven et al in a fascinating study with 28 subjects with intellectual disability ranging in age from 18 to 66 in the Netherlands. They stated: "The unstable mood disorder in the present paper resembles the description of the ICD-10 diagnosis of cyclothymia (F34.0) (Verhoeven et al., 2001): p.152).

In their study results Verhoeven et al 2001 concluded: "Valproic acid was prescribed in 28 subjects within a dose range of 300 to 3000 mg. per day. No major side effects were observed." They found moderate to marked improvement in 19 participants. Improvement included stabilization of behavior and mood, and a reduction of symptoms belonging to the mood, anxiety, and motor domains.

(Note: Valproic acid, Valproex sodium, and Depakote are different names for an equivalent anticonvulsant medication).

### Treatment considerations:

1.  Cyclothymic disorder is a milder form of a bipolar disorder spectrum disorder. It is a medical problem like child onset diabetes, ADHD, and heart disease. Treatment with mood stabilizers or low doses of anticonvulsant medication may often be a starting point for the medical treatment of these young people. Be sure to talk to your doctors and pharmacists about side effects and interactions of prescribed medications with drugs such as antidepressants, psychostimulants, pain medications or codeine products.
2.  Young people with cyclothymic disorder experience considerable anxiety and frustration in their family, school, and interpersonal lives. They need encouragement, firm and consistent guidance, mentors, and moral instruction to emphasize respect for others and their feelings and beliefs. Child and family therapy can emphasize appropriate expression of feelings, boundaries, limit setting, self-control, and coping skills. Parents need to 'be in charge' of these demanding and sometimes difficult children.

3. A close working relationship with the school is crucial for the child to succeed. Parents need to meet regularly (at least once a month) with the teacher or key teachers at the beginning of the year so that everyone understands what is expected of the child or teen. Everyone needs to be clear on what these students are capable of achieving. Periodic psychological and psychiatric evaluations will support the parent and teachers' efforts to guide the child and maximize her opportunity to learn.

4. Social skills are important to fitting in with peers. Simultaneously, these children need to manage their social anxiety. Educational planning to address these concerns early in the school year can make the difference between success and failure for your child. Small counseling/social skills groups with structured activities to address these concerns are helpful. After school social activities help increase their comfort with others.

5. In addition, psycho-pharmacologists are finding that the mood stabilizer medications, anticonvulsant (GABA) medications are often effective in treating social anxiety. It may be that hypomania and social anxiety are related. The most effective treatment approach is usually a combination of counseling and medication.

**Summary:**

- Cyclothymic disorder encourages rapid mood changes, rapid thinking, and impulsive, restless behavior. These moods and behaviors may cause problems, disruption in a tightknit school class or community.

- For parents and teachers to fully understand these moody students, a school psychologist or psychologist needs to administer personality and psychological inventories and behavior checklists. In this way these often reserved, shy students can express themselves in helpful ways. In ways they may not usually express themselves during an interview or in public.

- Having these students draw or write poems is another helpful way to express themselves appropriately. It helps them to share information with important adults in their lives.
- Children or students with behavioral problems frequently have sleep disorders, mood and stress disorders that need to be assessed. Once these mental health disorders are identified, treatment and helpful intervention can occur at a clinic, school and at home.

*Chapter 6*

# Assessment and Intervention in School

---

Assessment of Cyclothymic disorder can be a complex, step by step process to gather enough information to make an accurate diagnosis. The mental health practitioner needs to have an effective strategy and work with a team of persons who are well acquainted with the student to gather such information. Over the years this mental health provider found the following principles to be helpful and effective in working with mood disordered students.

**Principles of Effective Assessment of the Cyclothymic Student include:**

- Use multiple observers and informants to collect information
- Use different assessment instruments to capture the multi-dimensions of this medical illness
- Involve family members who observe the student frequently
- Involve teachers and other school professionals in assessment
- Actively engage the cyclothymic student in the assessment process.
- Use a variety of activities to motivate students to participate in assessment to encourage changes and objectives they and their family desire.

**Complete Assessment Will Include Measurement of the Presence and Severity of:**

- Hypomanic mood with its excessive energy, restless mind and body, with irritability, impaired concentration and impaired judgment. Young students may show hyperactive behavior, rush through tasks, and may have an inability to focus on one task. Older students may show irritable mood, racing thoughts with rapid speech.

- Depressive mood may be mild or severe and encourages avoidance of others and discourages motivation to complete tasks. Depressive episodes and avoidance of others is more common by puberty and middle school.

- Disruptive, erratic sleep patterns that include insomnia, and result in fatigue, lack of concentration, distractibility, and sleepiness in the classroom. Difficulty going to sleep and waking between 2 and 4 a.m. signals the presence of hypomanic mood with racing thoughts.

- Externalizing behavior including arguments and conflict with others, aggressive behavior, conduct problems, impulsive behavior, risk-taking behavior, and such behaviors as stealing, fire-setting, and cruelty towards animals and other people.

- Mood swings: Rapid, unpredictable mood changes where the student is happy one minute and minutes later she may be angry, hostile, and/or be aggressive in speech and action.

- Taking careful family medical, mental health and mood history to examine genetic and personality factors that may encourage a mood disorder in this student. Asking about previous hospitalizations of family members for mental health reasons and suicide attempts of family members will add important evidence towards making this diagnosis.

## The Assessment the Cyclothymic Student

### There is a Need to Work Closely with Parents

When a parent calls me for an appointment with concerns about their child performing poorly at school, having no motivation for school work, nor wanting to go to school, this psychologist requests that they bring along any achievement testing scores, grade cards, IQ testing results, and any notes from the teacher expressing concern about her or his student. Sometimes the parent reports that the school psychologist or a children's hospital has tested and evaluated her child. The parent is encouraged to bring those evaluation or report results. These reports provide important information and clues as to the student's struggles at school and elsewhere.

During the first meeting, this psychologist typically interviews the parents separately to obtain a history of the problem, what treatment has been attempted, to discuss what medications have been tried and what have been the results of treatment. How satisfied are the parents with past assessment, evaluations of their child? Were those evaluations parsimonious, economical, complete, and informative? Did past testing and assessment help guide the parent and Cyclothymic student in treatment?

Usually twenty minutes or more are spent in taking a family mental health history including a thorough history of mood disorders in the family. The following treatment specialists and researchers recommend taking time for such medical history as it provides important diagnostic information: (Akiskal, et al., 2005; Akiskal et al., 2000; Akiskal & Downs, 1985; Algorta et al., 2011; Garfinkel & Golombek, 1983; Papolos & Papolos, 2002; Shea, 2009). See Reference section for details.

**Family History Questions**

Questions and topics discussed with parents and guardians include:

- Have parents, grandparents, aunts, uncles or other relatives dealt with depressive episodes and problems? Been hospitalized for such mood problems?
- Have parents or other family members had periods of nervous, hyperactive/energetic mood or periods of great restlessness? Have family members, relatives been hospitalized for a "nervous breakdown?" or anxiety, stress?
- Does a parent, an aunt or uncle, or other family member have problems going to sleep, waking frequently, or having work or school problems related to sleep? Are there sleep deprivation problems present in the family?
- Do one or more relatives of your student have mood swings?

- Has a family member or relative used alcohol or drugs excessively and become violent or aggressive when using substances?

Answers to these questions are noted at the beginning of each psychological report. This history is forwarded to the treating physician, psychiatrist, mental health provider, and with the parent's permission, to the school IEP team.

The parents are given several child behavior checklists and rating scales to complete including: Child Behavior Checklist for Ages 4 – 18 (CBCL for Ages 4 -18), the N I C H Q Vanderbilt Assessment Scale – Parent Informant and the Conners' Rating Scales (CPRS-48).These assessment tools provide needed information on behavior at home, chore and schoolwork behaviors, on how this student relates with parents and siblings. They describe mood changes, sleep behavior, health concerns, and problems with thinking and concentration. The evaluating psychologist, the school IEP team, and the treatment team can review summaries of this behavior, ratings, and profiles to reach conclusions on possible diagnoses, intervention, and treatment directions.

This procedure of gathering parental information allows for important comparison and confirmation of students' behaviors and mood signs and symptoms. By doing such data collection and comparing data from parents and teachers, the psychologist and psychiatrist can be ascertained that he or she is on track to arriving a more accurate diagnosis.

**Using Multiple Informants**

Teachers, school psychologists, and school counselors *along with parents* and school administrators are at the frontline of assessing the cyclothymic student, whether he or she is a child or a teenager.

Teachers are a valuable source of information. Over the years, they have willingly completed the *Teacher's Report Form for Ages 5-18* of *the Child Behavior Checklist (CBCL 4-18)* to provide needed data to diagnose students with a mood disorder. They provide data on grades in subjects, how appropriately the child is behaving, and how much he/she is learning. They usually describe in detail what concerns them most about this student. They describe the best things about this pupil.

The *Teacher's Report Form (TRF)* has the teacher rate the frequency of such classroom behavior as inability to concentrate, disruptive behavior, ability to get along with other students, anxious behavior, responsible behavior, changes in mood, loud or talkative behavior. This data is graphed on a *TRF Profile for Boys – Problem Scales and a TRF Profile for Girls- Problems Scales*. This profile has 3 sections: Internalizing Behavior, A Social Problem/ Thought Problems/Attention Dimension and an Externalizing Behavior Problem dimension.

Researchers are finding that this assessment data, along with mood measures and family mental health and mood history, is helpful in identifying mood disordered and Cyclothymic youth. School psychologists provide a valuable service with standardized testing of student achievement, ratings of their behavior in the classroom, and IQ testing with related behavior and temperament observations.

Achievement test results, behavioral observations, mood reports from teacher and school personnel are useful for in assessing the mood disordered student. This information can be combined with the Millon Personality Inventories data and anxiety and mood inventories ratings for effective and complete assessment. Parent behavior ratings and checklists are added to this data bank to guide careful diagnosis of students.

## Addressing Thoughts of Self-Harm:

This psychologist encouraged children to draw and write during our interviews. Pictures often show their view of self, how they cope with others, and permit them to share feelings of anxiety, sadness and anger. Sometimes aggressive behavior or self-harm feelings are clearly pictured in their drawings. See the following example.

One sixth grade boy drew a picture of himself with wounds, marks, blood pouring out of his mouth, his eyes shut and his head hanging to the side as if he had hung himself. He wrote curse words on his body, and they suggested that he had sad feelings, low self-worth, and strong feelings of self-depreciation. A short poem that he wrote had the words: "I'm not cool. I'm not happy. I want to die." He wrote other words expressing strong feelings: angry, curse words. He was a wounded boy.

This psychologist spoke with his mother separately regarding needed psychiatric treatment. He and his mother were immediately referred to a treating psychiatrist for medical evaluation and evaluation of his mood disorder and suicidal thinking. We go into detail in the assessment and treatment of suicidal depression in Chapter 9.

## Case Studies That Highlight Different Issues

### Case of a Nervous, Socially Anxious Elementary School Student

Tommy, age 9, came with his maternal grandmother, Marcia, for assessment and treatment. Marcia commented: "He's high-strung, restless and used to no rules." She reported that he's been calling other students names on the bus and has been fighting on the playground. He faced school suspension.

He was administered the WISC-III and obtained average Verbal Scores on oral Arithmetic and Digit Span. The tests involve concentration in calculation of math problems and recalling a string of numbers. Tommy was motivated during testing, stood up during much of the testing, and showed fidgety and restless behavior. He used effective, self-verbalizations to solve some problems.

His grandmother and his teacher completed child behavior checklists.

The Conners' Rating Scales indicated problems with sleep, fears and worry, restless behavior and temper outbursts. He had aggressive behavior, argued with others, and had problems keeping friends.

His grandmother and teacher completed behavior checklists (*CBCL/parent form and CBCL/teacher report form/TRF*). These Report forms indicated that Tommy had problems with concentration, cruel or mean behavior, risk-taking behavior, and being too fearful. He was described as a nervous, high-strung, tense, and disobedient student. His checklist profile and his signs and symptoms pointed toward a child with a Cyclothymic mood disorder with related sleep, social anxiety, and behavioral problems.

## This Student Needed Immediate Help from an IEP Team

Tommy's mother and his grandmother were encouraged to work closely with the school Intervention team. A key IEP team member, whether a school counselor or school psychologist who has good rapport with Tommy may talk with Tommy about such important issues: "When does he feel nervous or tense during the school day?" "When does he notice that he gets loud or gets grouchy, mad, or irritable?" "What helps you to stay or feel calm?"

By encouraging school IEP members to have weekly talks with Tommy and with his mother or grandmother, they may arrive at directions for helpful school interventions, and for treatment suggestions to his treatment providers. Often giving the child a counseling activity break for managing stress is helpful. Playing a game like the Talking, Feeling, and Doing game, helps the child release tension and feel more accepted.

This provider recommended that mother, grandmother, and Tommy work with a child psychologist and child psychiatrist familiar with treating mood disorders in children.

Dr. David Perlmutter, a neurologist, recommends nutritional treatment of attention and mood problems. He describes how malnutrition and eating wheat, carbs, and sugar in our meals encourages health problems, inflammation in the body, hyperactivity, ADHD, and depression. (Perlmutter, 2013). Parents and treatment providers are encouraged to examine his writing of how brain functioning is improved by healthy eating choices and habits. Chapter 7 goes into detail on this subject.

This next case of an intelligent teenager illustrates how well she was able to identify *when her mood signs and symptoms began* during childhood and her middle school years.

## Assessment Example of Marie, a Bright, Precocious, Frustrated 15- Year-Old Student

With Marie, a bright teenager, this practitioner used a combination of standardized tools including the Wechsler Intelligence Scale for Children – Fourth Edition (WISC-IV) to assess her Verbal Comprehension, Perceptual Reasoning, her Working Memory and Processing Speed. We wanted to see how her intelligence influenced her achievement, her personal relations, and how her mood and sleep patterns influenced her reasoning and her concentration.

Marie had been treated with Concerta for a possible ADHD diagnosis. Her mother commented: "We tried this medication during fifth grade, and it didn't help. We saw no change." Chief complaints included: "Teachers' are commenting that she is not putting forth the effort." Marie stated: "I can't finish tests."

Family mental health history found a maternal uncle who was "probably ADHD" and a paternal uncle being bipolar.

Marie's mother completed the *NICHQ Vanderbilt Assessment Scale –Parent Informant,* and reported that Marie does not pay attention to details and does not listen when spoken to directly. Marie fails to finish activities, often has difficulty organizing tasks and loses things needed for tasks. She blames others for her mistakes. Reading and writing are somewhat of a problem.

When Marie's mother completed *the CBCL Behavior Checklist for Ages 4-18 (CBCL)*and the *Conner's Rating Scales (CPRS-48),* we'd collected more information, more pieces to the puzzle of what was blocking Marie's achievement in school. The *CBCL* brought out that Marie performed above average in Arithmetic and Science, and below average in Reading, English and Spanish. Her mother observed that she has had trouble turning in assignments and finishing tests since the 4th grade.

Key behaviors observed on the *CBCL* included: gets distracted, fidgeting, not completing tasks when asked (at home), feels nervous and tense. Mother reported that she is secretive, is compulsive in arranging things in order, and has *sudden changes in mood*. The *Conners Rating Scales* provided more useful information. Marie is observed to "pretty much" be sassy with adults, wants to run things, does not listen, and daydreams.

Marie completed the *Youth Self-Report (YSR) for Ages 11-18* of the *CBCL*, the *Beck Anxiety Inventory, the Mood Questionnaire*, and the *WISC-IV* intelligence test for ages 6 to 16. Marie was an excellent reporter on the *YSR* and stated that sometimes she argues a lot, fails to finish things, has trouble sitting still, and feels confused. She is afraid of the dark, feels a need to be perfect, and is nervous or tense (since age 12). As they age and mature, some pre-teens and teenagers become more nervous or self-conscious, shy, and anxious during middle and high school.

Marie added on the YSR that she can be pretty friendly, works well with her hands, likes to make others laugh. She commented about being easily distracted: "I just zone out and daydream randomly." "I have been inattentive and distracted forever". Key clues included that she has been louder than other kids since age 5; has worried a lot since age 10; and has had trouble sleeping since age 13. She commented: "I just keep thinking and have trouble falling asleep".

**WISC-IV Testing Results Guided My Choices of Assessment Tools**

Administering the *Wechsler Intelligence Scale for Children (WISC-IV)* can be an enjoyable experience. Marie was administered the *WISC-IV*, and this psychologist enjoyed engaging her in this examination. She was motivated in working with colored blocks and placing them in pictured designs. She worked rapidly and scored well on this test. Marie scored well on Verbal Comprehension with an excellent Composite score of 114 and a Perceptual Reasoning score of 117. Her Average scores of 97 on Working

Memory, typified a young lady with a busy, distractible mind, her scaled score of 91 on Processing Speed reflected an anxious, compulsive mind and personality.

Her Vocabulary score was in the gifted range, so I decided to administer the *Mood Questionnaire* by Robert M.A. Hirschfeld, M.D. to see how well she could describe her mood states and symptoms. Marie stated that she had felt so hyper that other people thought she was not her normal self since age 12. She felt irritable, started arguments, and got much less sleep than usual since age 12. She observed that thoughts raced through her head, and she could not slow her mind down since age 13; was easily distracted, had trouble staying on track, and always had much more energy than usual.

She checked 10 of 13 symptoms of hypomanic mood and stated she had several of these during the same time period. Marie rated her restless, manic mood on the Mood Disorder Questionnaire as a moderate problem in general and at school. This result suggested she had a Cyclothymic disorder.

**Conclusions and Favorable Use of Test Results**

This evaluator believed this example of Marie represents a complete, parsimonious examination of this young lady's concerns and problems with the full cooperation of mother and Marie. Teacher observations were shared indirectly.

Mother requested a report for her pediatrician to treat her primary diagnosis of Cyclothymic disorder. This report was mailed to him with the intent of making her life easier by stabilizing her mood changes, and reducing her nervous, anxious mood. This psychologist recommended the treatment of both her mood and sleep disorders.

## Intervention and Treatment Principles

It is prudent for the psychologist, school psychologist, the school IEP team, and the student's treatment team to follow treatment principles and guidelines that ensure that the Cyclothymic student receives prompt and effective treatment from medical providers, mental health providers, and school personnel. Such treatment will prevent harm to self and to others and ensure that the student can achieve like his peers.

1.  When the student is ascertained and diagnosed with cyclothymic mood, prompt evaluation and treatment of *hypomanic mood* is needed. Some teenagers use marijuana to self-medicate this 'nervous' mood'.
2.  Sleep problems need to be addressed immediately and not 6 months into the school year. Parents, the student, the IEP team, and treatment providers need to assess the possibility of sleep disorders. Sleep charting, sleep diaries, and sleep studies are recommended to evaluate and effectively treat mood disorders and learning disordered students. (Papolos and Papolos, 1999).
3.  When the Cyclothymic student shifts to depressed mood due to their motivation to be with others and engage in schoolwork is decreased greatly. Parents, teachers, treatment providers need to intervene to determine what will help the student move on from this depressed episode. A combination of medical treatment and counseling is recommended.
4.  The importance of teacher, school counselor and school psychologist's reports and letters about student's behavior and school performance can't be underestimated. These observations along with IEP team reports, and letters from administrators are helpful in guiding medical and mental health treatment for these students.
5.  We need to keep in mind that the consistent thing about these students is that they are inconsistent in their behavior, moods, concentration, and schoolwork. Regular, periodic teamwork among parents, teachers, students, and treatment providers helps these students tremendously.

John A. Paulus PhD

## How Effective, Comprehensive Assessment Guided Prompt Medical Treatment for a 15-Year-Old Mood Disordered Teen

Owen, age 15, was an engaging, personable, and intelligent young man. He and his parents were motivated for change and for treatment. His mother listed the following concerns on the *CBCL for Ages 4-18*: "He's never happy until he beats the video game, He works himself into a frenzy with this game." She reported he had a D average for grades and when he puts forth any effort his grades improve. "He doesn't like being told what to do."

On the *CBCL behavior checklist* she described the following behaviors as often true: argues a lot, fears going to school, bites his fingernails, and is nervous. His mother described him as high strung or tense, being too fearful or anxious, having poor schoolwork, and refusing to talk. It's often true that Owen is stubborn, irritable, sulks a lot, and has sudden mood changes.

### Owen's Self-report:

Owen completed the *CBCL Youth Self-Report for Ages 11-18 (YSR)*. He disliked sports. He reported that Zoloft, an antidepressant medication, "did nothing." He stated that "I'm up during the weekends until 4 a.m. to play games online." He reported that his psychiatrist increased the Zoloft dosage and this medication did not help his sleep. He reported having 4 or more friends.

On the YSR he described the following behaviors and feelings:

"It is often true that 'I argue a lot', have trouble concentrating, and am mean to others. I do not feel guilty after doing something I shouldn't, and, I bite my fingernails. It is often true that I would rather be alone, and my school work is poor". He reported that he sometimes stays up real late, refuses to do things, has a hot temper with anyone, and feels unhappy or depressed.

**PMI Administration With Both Parents.**

The Paulus Mood Inventory (PMI) was used to assess the presence of a "mood swing disorder or a Cyclothymic disorder. Both parents answered questions and rated their son's mood problems.

Owen's mother identified with some of the signs and symptoms her son showed and reported that 'she had sleep problems and could be vocal or stubborn also'. She found that he was often "nervous or uncomfortable with groups", often sensitive, shy with others, and is easily sidetracked. She observed him complaining of being tired or bored, having sudden changes in mood, getting angry and irritable, being nervous, and having trouble sleeping at night (like she does). She rated him as having a total score of 74 which indicated a mood swing problem and a likelihood of a Cyclothymic disorder.

Owen's father rated many of the same signs and symptoms at a lower frequency, and as being present some of the time. It is possible that he had less opportunity to observe his son's behavior due to work responsibilities.

He saw his son having no interest in outdoor activities, and saw him getting angry easily, getting stubborn or irritable, and sometimes having crying spells. His father observed him getting angry with video games when Owen was not able to do well. He rated him as having a total score of 44.

**Personality Inventory for Children (PIC)**

This standardized personality inventory was commonly used in the 1990's and 2000's and gave the psychologist data on personality factors, validity factors as to the honesty and openness of the rater. The student is rated on depression, anxiety, and his relations with others. Owen's mother completed this personality inventory and Owen obtained significant ratings on Social Incompetence, Psychological Maladjustment (T score of 80), poor Adjustment (T score of 75), Depression (T score of 85),

Withdrawal (T score of 80), Psychological Disturbance/Avoidance of others (T score of 105). T scores of 75 and above are clinically significant.

## Conclusions and Treatment Direction for Owen

Owen and his parents had been working with treating psychiatrists at a nearby hospital for two years. His mental health and his schoolwork were not improving and getting worse. It was apparent to us that his hypomanic mood, his mood swings, his erratic sleep and his periodic depression were getting the better of him. We concluded that he had a Cyclothymic disorder or mild to moderate manic-depressive illness.

We constructed a new treatment plan and direction. His parents requested that I send my testing results, and my complete evaluation with my diagnosis and treatment recommendations to his treating psychiatrist. Owen was started on a low dose of anti-convulsant medication. A few weeks later a mild dose of a neuroleptic medication was added to treat his sleep problems. With treatment Owen was able to manage his mood swings, improve his sleep patterns and his concentration, His school work improved along with his motivation. By careful gathering of diagnostic information, the four of us were able to find a solution to Owen's problems.

**The next student case example had a longer medical, psychiatric treatment history. Therefore, we were able to move more quickly based on past, available medical treatment information.**

Steve, a motivated teen and his father had a good working relationship and their rapport and ability to listen and respect one another made this case a solvable one.

## Treatment and IEP for a Teenager with a Cyclothymic Disorder, Social Anxiety, Insomnia and Introversion.

Steve, age 17, and his father were seen because his father was concerned with Steve earning 'bad grades', not liking to be on time for school, forgetting what he reads, and finding 'school to be boring'. School went well for Steve until the fourth grade when his father observed that "ADD showed up like a passion!" He had been treated for ADD by a psychiatrist for several years. His father commented that Steve has had tremendous insomnia, sleep problems since age 10 when he started Ritalin, a psychostimulant medication.

School concerns included declining grades the last two years and a refusal to turn in his schoolwork. Steve reported that he forgets what he reads. He stated: "I forget everything in a minute." He added: "I usually have to read it four times and I still forget it later." He complained that algebra homework takes him "forever to complete" and that he gets distracted doing it.

With administration of the WISC-III test, we found Steve to have superior verbal reasoning with a Similarities scaled score of 18; however, he scored low on a verbal test of concentration earning a scaled score of 7 on Digit Span. A scaled score of 10 is average.

**Medical Treatment:**

Clinical history, diagnostic interviews with Steve and his father, and the *CBCL Youth Self-Report* gave indication that Steve had a mood disorder, a Cyclothymic Disorder with related social anxiety, introversion, and depressive signs. He had difficulty concentrating, and extra sensitivity to environment and criticism. Steve saw his treating psychiatrist and was started on an anticonvulsant, mood stabilizer medication.* His father reported a good response to medication as Steve became less depressed, less moody and began to socialize.

*Note: Anticonvulsant medication is processed by the liver and doesn't always work well for some students. Sometimes neuroleptic medication, mild dose, or another medication will need to be tried to treat a mood swing disorder to stabilize it.

As Steve's mood was stabilized, we were able to move on to the next phase of treatment and examined what Steve could do at school to increase his repertoire of social-emotional skills. We wanted to bring Steve up to speed with his EQ, his emotional quotient, so that he could better socialize with peers, reduce conflict, and reduce his use of emotional energy. Students with mood swings exhaust their emotional energy, and go home to take naps. We wanted Steve to learn to conserve his emotional energy with more efficient coping skills. We wanted to see him blend in with peers.

**School Intervention**

This clinician was fortunate at that time to be able to refer to excellent school interventions and IEP protocols offered by Papolos and Papolos (1999, 2002). The following IEP was constructed for Steve for use at school:

Goal 1: Steve will learn and apply strategies to independently divert negative or oppositional thoughts.

Objectives:

A. Steve will explore negative thoughts with his school counselor or therapist and develop strategies for diverting them.
B. Steve will tell an appropriate adult when he has 'bad' thoughts he can't manage.
C. Steve will use a variety of learned strategies and document results in a journal at least 2 times a week.

Goal 2: Steve will develop different ways to manage anxiety and stress rather than resort to the use of harmful, unproductive behaviors.

Objectives:

A. When faced with a stressful situation, Steve will examine his choices with his counselor/therapist.

B. Steve will talk to a supportive adult when he feels explosive or he is losing control.

Goal 3: Steve will increase his communication skills in a variety of settings.

Objectives:

A. Steve will practice using communication skills at least one time per week with school staff and by writing in his journal.
B. Steve will converse in a positive manner with a peer three times a week.

Goal 4: Steve will decrease explosive, impulsive behavior and increase his ability to manage anger, his patience and feelings of frustration.

Objectives:

A. Steve will learn to recognize early signs of impending hypomanic or depressive mood cycle. He will talk about these episode signs with his treating psychiatrist, psychologist, or therapist.
B. Steve will earn points for doing any of the above. Points can be used for having a day without homework, or doing something special that motivates this student. Supervised social activity is recommended.

**Summary:**

1. Each student is unique. Each Cyclothymic student is unique and has her own personality, talents, anxieties, mood, and sleep patterns. It takes a caring, concerned adult to listen and to discover their needs, their stressors, and what they need specifically for guidance and treatment. As with Steve, assume the student will be responsible to follow treatment guidelines and suggestions. Yet encourage and monitor them on a continual basis, daily at first, then weekly.

2.  It takes creativity, flexibility, and experience for the counselor, teacher, school psychologist, parent, or treatment provider to connect with the Cyclothymic student to encourage sharing of concerns. By being optimistic, the caring adult can help the student express himself with a drawing activity, drawing a cartoon, playing a brief game to relax the teenager or child. When the student feels acceptance and feels safe, he will share what he wants different, and you the helper are half-way to solving the problem.

3.  Have a specific treatment and goal in mind. Involve and include support people, intervention team members, parents, and brief consults with the treatment provider. The team can help the student find answers to his or her dilemma and help them reduce stress.

4.  Students, including the cyclothymic student, want change and want to know that their lives can be better. We can use resources like Seligman, M. (2007) in working with challenged, moody students. We need to give these students hope and encourage them by stating: "Change can happen with work, your continued daily effort, and with allowing others to work with us."

# Chapter 7

# Nutrition for a Healthy Mind and Body

---

## Introduction

During the past 10 years researchers are finding increasing evidence that overconsumption of carbohydrate foods, sugar, and gluten are causing neurological problems, depression, and gastro-intestinal problems. These problems disturb the mood, sleep, concentration and learning of students. Nutritional experts found that consuming natural fats, protein, and probiotic foods lead to increased energy, better concentration and brain function and calmer bodies and minds.

Dr. Reuben lost his father to colon cancer. He went of a mission to find out how people in African and Asian countries ate to avoid heart disease, gastrointestinal diseases, and cancer. He and his wife developed nutrition plans and recipes including use of bran flakes in meals to increase fiber in the diet. These meals helped eliminate gastro-intestinal problems, cleanse the intestinal tract, and keep that system healthy. (Reuben, 1975).

Bieler (1965), Perlmutter (2013, 2015), and Fife (2019) recommend nutrition to keep our minds, our bodies healthy, and to keep us energetic, in better mental health and mood. Garfinkel and Golombek reviewed the literature for factors encouraging suicidal behavior in adolescence. They found that a high percentage of adolescent suicide attempters had physical complaints for which no diagnosis had been made, and that male suicide attempters had a greater prevalence of somatic complaints, particularly gastrointestinal complaints than matched psychiatric control adolescents. (Garfinkel & Golombek, 1983). We can only guess what these male students consumed during the day and evening to upset their digestive systems.

What we eat affects our mood and our sense of feeling well. Avoiding harmful foods that encourage inflammation in our bodies takes guidance from nutritional experts.

## Modern Eating Habits are Harming Our Brains

David Perlmutter, neurologist, and fellow of nutrition, wrote two books on nutrition and explained how modern nutritional, eating practices encourage inflammation in our bodies and brains and cause many illnesses. He explained that we eat too much wheat, carbs, and sugar, and we eat too little natural fat. Gluten, carbohydrate foods can cause grave problems with our gastro-intestinal system, and weaken our immunity for arthritis, dementia, and encourage depression and other illnesses. (Perlmutter, 2015, 2013).

Thousands of years ago our ancestors ate fats that made up 75% of their diet, ate protein from meat and nuts to make up 20% of their diet, and carbs made up 5% of their diet. The diet recommended by U.S. experts in recent years, according to Dr. Perlmutter, was 60 % Carbs, 20% Protein, and 20% fat. As Americans followed this direction, we increased our rates of heart disease, diabetes, ADHD, anxiety, depression, insomnia, dementia, inflammation in the gut and other neurological symptoms.

Dr. Perlmutter reported that studies are describing Alzheimer's as a third type of diabetes beginning in 2005. Newer studies are showing a link between poor diet and Alzheimer's (Roberts et al., (2012), www.doctoroz.com/videos/alzheimer-diabetes-brain).

## Traditional Meals in Europe

As a young boy, I grew up in Holland, in a country with Holstein cows producing thousands of gallons of milk and large amounts of a different delicious cheeses. My home stood near several farms. My mother, 'Aaltje', learned to be a good cook for five children and our family of seven. She fixed us "boere kool", farmer's kale by boiling partially skinned, chopped potatoes and during the final minute of cooking, she added shredded kale. She drained these vegetables and mashed them together. The kale and potato dish served with gravy, a piece of polish sausage, and sauerkraut, made for a hearty and filling meal. Sauerkraut is fermented cabbage and is a favorite dish in Holland, Germany, and other Northern European countries.

This mental health provider learned years later from David Bieler MD that raw and cooked vegetables and raw goat's milk are healthy for our internal organs including our liver, and they encourage healing. Dr. David Perlmutter, M.D. wrote *Brain Maker* and described the benefits of probiotic, fermented foods. He wrote in detail how we can manage depression, ADHD, prevent dementia and inflammation of the brain and gut, with a meal plan high in natural fats with some natural protein foods complimented with such probiotic foods as yogurt, kefir, or a coconut water lemonade. (Bieler, 1965, Perlmutter, 2015).

Perlmutter spelled out how natural and Omega-3 fats and probiotic foods (like yogurt, sauerkraut) keep our gastro-intestinal systems healthy and prevent inflammation. These foods support the billions of healthy bacteria in our microbiome system located in our small intestine and colon. We can prevent diabetes, heart disease, mood, and attentional problems by eating such foods. We will discuss this science in more detail toward the end of this chapter.

## Mood States and Eating Behavior

When this psychologist began practicing in a hospital clinic with teenagers and families, he came across an excellent book on depression written by Demetri Papolos, M.D. and Janice Papolos. They wrote about appetite and major depression. They stated that major depression encourages severe disturbance in appetite and sleep patterns. "Usually a person complains of having no appetite – food just doesn't taste good anymore."(Papolos and Papolos 1997) : p.12.)

In their guide, *The Bipolar Child,* Papolos and Papolos describe bipolar children and adolescents as having "an insatiable appetite for carbohydrates and sweets." They asked one 20-year-old woman who suffered with bipolar disorder if she ever craved sweets and carbohydrates *as a child.* She reported eating a gallon of ice cream every evening. (Papolos and Papolos, 1999, 2002): p. 19

Perugi, et al,2006 investigated the relationship between bulimia nervosa and atypical depression. They found that cyclothymic temperament, related mood reactivity, and interpersonal sensitivity may account for much of the relationship between bulimia and atypical depression. McElroy et al, 2005 reviewed the literature for the relationship of bipolar disorders and eating disorders. They found that epidemiological studies showed an association between subthreshold bipolar disorders and eating disorders in adolescents. These mood disorders include cyclothymic disorders.

**Dramatic Energy Changes**

Papolos and Papolos observed that the bipolar child or the mood swing child can have dramatic energy switches in a single day. This provider wondered what causes such energy changes. We do not have cameras in our children's bedrooms to record or video tape their eating and grazing habits. Some parents shared during evaluations, that their children will leave snack wrappers littered in their bedrooms, and sometimes hide wrappers under a mattress. Snacking on candy bars, carbohydrate treats could be one possible culprit. It would be worthwhile for parents and mental health workers to inquire more into the eating habits of mood disorder children and youth.

Fife (2017) observed increased energy with adult patients when they changed their diets and added virgin coconut oil to their meals, cooking, and salads. By adding more natural fat to their diets, adults improved their health and energy and lost weight. With the erratic behavior and moods of the Cyclothymic student, is it possible that their continual changes in eating practices encourage their energy changes?

Little research exists on the foods consumed by cyclothymic students and how their eating patterns influence their energy states during the day or night. My hunch follows the lead of Perlmutter (2015) and Fife (2017) that overconsumption of carbohydrates, sugar, artificial sweeteners, and mass-produced vegetable oils in snacks and meals may be causing serious problems in the digestive tract. Such eating practices alter the neurochemical production in the gut.

Drs. Perlmutter and Fife described serious inflammatory disease from such eating habits. These carbohydrate foods, vegetable oil cooked foods, and sweeteners may inflame the bodies and brains of students. They may become depressed, distractible, or periodically wound up. They may not be able to calm their minds and bodies to relax and rest at night, nor concentrate to study. Research is needed in this area with these Cyclothymic students.

**Improving Attention and Memory**

Perlmutter reported that curcumin, the main active ingredient in turmeric, has been used in traditional Chinese and Indian medicine for thousands of years. It has an ability to increase BDNF in the brain. This protein, or 'brain-derived neurotrophic factor' plays an important role in creating new brain cells or neurons. It can help prevent or slow the development of Alzheimer's, depression, obsessive-compulsive disorder, and other neuro-degenerative illnesses. (Perlmutter, 2013).

Dr. Perlmutter stated that scientists are increasingly studying, DHA, docosahexaenoic acid, a critical brain fat. It makes up one-fourth of the fat in the human brain. This brain fat (DHA) helps to regulate inflammation. "It can block damaging effects of a high-sugar diet." Dr. Perlmutter stated that many kids are not getting enough DHA today. He believes that is "why we are seeing so many cases of attention deficit hyperactivity disorder (ADHD)." He reported that he has cured cases of ADHD with recommending the DHA (brain fat) supplement. He advised taking 200 to 300 milligrams daily. (Perlmutter, 2013): 141.

This person wondered if DHA may help treat cyclothymic disordered students with distractibility as well. We need to investigate and research this possibility.

## Sleep

Cyclothymic and Bipolar children have difficulty getting up, report sleepiness and low energy and poor concentration in the morning and greater sleep disturbance than their peers ((Papolos and Papolos, (1999); Van Meter et al., (2013); Van Meter et al., (2011)).

This psychologist heard from parents of children diagnosed with cyclothymic disorder that these children had great difficulty going to sleep due to an increase of energy in the evenings. Their minds were more active, restless, and energetic in the evening. These students were more excitable and played video games, texted, talked to friends into the late evenings. Parents complained that their children were difficult to calm down in the evenings.

Family therapy and intervention involved going into detail on sleep hygiene practices. We looked at ways of providing a quiet, low light, low stimulating bedroom. No video or cell phones were permitted an hour before bedtime. We examined how their child or teen could design their bedroom, so it was more calming and relaxing for them.

Mood swing children and students have variable energy states, appetites, changing moods, and become more energetic and alert in the evenings. Perhaps it makes sense to have older cyclothymic, hyperthymic students attend school from 11 a.m. to 7 p.m. It may be a better match for their circadian rhythms. When only we can find teachers to work those hours! This change could happen this fall as some school districts are now planning online schooling for high school students.

Dr. Papolos reported on research by Dr. Thomas Wehr and colleagues at the National Institute of Mental Health with depressed, rapid-cycling bipolar patients. They found that patients who had one night of sleep deprivation switched into mania or hypomania the next day. Dr. Papolos recommended monitoring the sleep/wake cycle, and using sedative medication to encourage regular sleep cycles. Papolos and Papolos, (1999): 136.

## Good Natural Nutrition May Encourage Better Sleep

What the cyclothymic student or the sleep disordered student eats before he or she goes to bed makes a difference in calming the mind, the gut, and the body of your student. When your student follows healthy eating practices, they will have a healthy functioning gastro-intestinal system, and they become calmer. When they consume omega-3 fats, foods with fiber, and grass-fed animal beef, bison, lamb, and probiotic food, they may have calmer stomach, gut, and brain functioning to encourage restful sleep.

When students binge on sugar snacks, donuts, pizza, and hydrogenated vegetable oil foods and chips and fries, their stomachs, gut linings, and their brains can become inflamed. When minds and bodies are inflamed, upset, or distressed, sleep becomes erratic. Our bodies are not constructed to manage these "foreign foods" and become distressed. Perlmutter stated: "The good news is that we can reverse many of neurological, psychological, and behavioral disorders just by going gluten-free and adding supplements like DHA and probiotics to our diet." (Perlmutter, 2013): 155. Then sleep may come naturally.

In Chapter 3, Dr. Perlmutter described a case of a lady with a distressed, depressed belly. He evaluated and inquired:

- Had she been on antibiotics?
- Was she on a high carbohydrate diet?
- Did she have difficulty losing weight on a low-fat diet?
- What medication did she take for high cholesterol?
- Any medicine for gastro-intestinal disturbance or acid-reflux?
- Was she on any sleep medication?

When Dr. Perlmutter did his medical exam, his laboratory tests including tests for inflammatory markers, he knew this lady had a distressed gastro-intestinal system and her microbiome was sick.

In the ensuing weeks, Dr. Perlmutter changed her nutrition plan. Medications were tapered off and stopped over time. This lady's system began to reduce inflammation, increase production of healthy neurochemicals in her gut, and she became calmer, and her sleep patterns became normal. She lost extra weight. She was no longer depressed nor distressed. Perlmutter (2015): 71-72.

Too often our depressed, mood swing students with sleep problems are quickly medicated to manage their symptoms. Too often the results of using multiple medications to treat our students is not helpful. Treatment of mood and related sleep problems need to incorporate and use the latest guidance of the National Institute of Health (NIH) and the National Sleep Foundation.

Perlmutter and Fife have followed the latest research on nutrition and use this research to guide their practice of treating patients with health concerns. Their results are positive and successful. Sleep, energy, and mood improves with natural foods, eating healthy fats, and avoiding carbohydrates, gluten, and sugars that inflame our gastro-intestinal system. (Perlmutter (2015), Fife (2017).

### Most Families and Students are Behind the Nutrition Curve When They Follow the Traditional Nutrition Recommendations.

For many years physicians and some researchers believed that a diet low in saturated fat, cholesterol, high in carbohydrates, grains, potatoes, rice, wheat, and moderate in proteins such as beef, lamb, fish, and nuts was the ideal diet.

Yet in the last 10 to 20 years researchers found that consuming a high natural fat diet, eating a moderate amount of protein, and consuming a low carbohydrate diet encourages the most energy, and more weight loss on a consistent basis. Such healthful eating provides the best gastro-intestinal health, reduced risk of diabetes, and better mood. (JW. Lee etal., 2008; Maria Almond, 2013; Mayo Clinic, Jan. 12, 2015; Fife, 2017; and Perlmutter, 2015.)

Dr. Perlmutter recommends eating foods high in fiber and reduced in refined sugars to support the variety of healthy flora, bacteria the gut needs to protect the gut wall so it does not become "leaky". Healthy eating can reduce inflammation in the gastro-intestinal tract and elsewhere in the body.

## Good Fat, Better Mind

Perlmutter (2015) recommended eating good fats, Omega-3 fats, as found in fish and wild-grass fed animals, to boost brain function and to stop inflammation.

Dr Bruce Fife explains in detail the harmful effects of sugar, artificial sweeteners, and high fructose corn syrup and how they encourage obesity. He goes on to describe how vegetable oils are hydrogenated and are easily converted into trans fatty acids. He stated: "these (hydrogenated) fats can wreak havoc on thyroid, pituitary, and other glands involved in governing and controlling metabolism and body weight." (Fife, 2019): p.130.

Fife describes how healthy fats help the body be healthy, energetic, and maintain a good weight. He explains that bad fats and excess eating of carbohydrates cause such health problems as diabetes, hypothyroidism, obesity, chronic malnutrition, infections, pain problems. We can solve these problems with good nutritional practices. Fife and Perlmutter recommend using coconut oil and olive oil in cooking and meals to obtain the healthy fats your body needs for energy, good gut health and good brain functioning. (Fife, 2017, Perlmutter, 2015).

The previous researchers found that eating high carbohydrate diets, diet high in the glycemic index, consuming too much sugar, fructose, and eating too little natural fat in your diet, throws the whole microbiome, gut

77

system out of whack. Such eating practices encourages the student's brain to be activated, to be wired at nighttime, and sleep becomes an elusive friend much needed.

## Eating Healthy, Organic Fats

Dr. Bruce Fife in his nutrition guide, *The Coconut Ketogenic Diet* wrote about low-fat diets and that his patients fail to lose weight in that manner. He stated that low-fat diets do not work and promote weight gain. He cites the Framingham, Massachusetts 40- year study that had interesting results of "people who ate the most saturated fat, ate the most calories, weighed the least". (http://www.framinghamheartstudy.org.) (Fife, 2017): 7.

Fife learned from researching medical literature that coconut oil was used successfully to treat seriously ill hospital patients. He found that Pacific Island people lived on a diet of coconuts and coconut oil and had low rates of heart disease. When he purposefully encouraged his patients to consume higher fat, natural fats, and coconut oil in their diets, he began to see dramatic changes in health of his patients. (Fife, 2017): p. 8.

Dr. Fife listed 26 health conditions that may be helped by coconut oil, by consuming 2 tablespoonful of this oil per day, including these 6 problems related to mood, sleeping, and eating problems:

1. Digestive problems
2. Fatigue, lack of energy
3. Gum diseases
4. Insomnia
5. Nervousness/irritability
6. Overweight/obesity.

Dr. Fife discovered that his patients became healthier with eating natural fats including coconut oil. He instructed his patients to eat coconut oil instead of vegetable oils, had them eat fatty meats and full-fat dairy, and more vegetables. Patients were instructed to eat less carbohydrate-rich grains and cereals. They had better heart and bone health, had more energy, better blood sugar readings and lost weight. He now focuses his health practice on a coconut ketogenic nutritional plan and has more healthy, happy patients.

**Possible Answers to Mood and Sleep Problems**

1. Change to nutrition plan favoring Omega-3 fats and natural fats as 60% or more of your and your student's daily diet. Keep plant and meat protein at 30% of daily calories, and consume carbohydrate foods at 10 % or less of your student's daily diet. Excess weight, health problems can disappear.

2. Prepare foods as a family ahead of time. When you gather the family around the table in the evening, family members can be assigned tasks. For salads, younger children can tear up lettuce, romaine lettuce, kale, and other leaf items. Pre-teens and teenagers can cut carrots, onions, zucchini, tomatoes, olives, avocados. Avocado is a rich and healthy source of natural fat that gives family members energy to fuel the burning off extra pounds. Have your kids help to pick out healthy/oil salad dressings at the store.

3. Have family meetings to plan meals. Cereal for breakfast is a deadly dull, dangerous food for blood sugar, and has high sugar and carbohydrate content that may lead to obesity and diabetes. Family members can get on the computer to research healthy, natural, Omega-3 fats, protein foods to create new and better tasting breakfasts. Your family can enjoy making omelets with cage free brown eggs, chopped pieces of Polish pork kielbasa, or another favorite meat, and by pouring in shredded kale, chopped zucchini, onion, a little toasted gluten free bread into the mix. Season to taste.

Your family can prepare high fat, high protein, high energy breakfast ingredients the night before by placing chopped items in small containers in the refrigerator. Use them the next day to prepare a healthy breakfast.

4.   Plan on three or more family meetings per week in the evenings. Family members meet up to construct and make their healthy, nutritional drinks for the next school day or workday. Fruits can be defrosted or made into juice, and added to water to make good tasting drinks. Make smoothies in your blender. Prepare frozen fruit, water, coconut milk, other milks, bananas, sliced or thawed mango, berries, and a favorite vegetable to make a flavorful smoothie. Taste test before taking with you in a thermos.

     Note: Avoid drinking diet colas or sugared drinks that encourage obesity, and internal health problems.

5.   Have quiet, relaxing, drawing, meditation, yoga, stretching, writing, reading activities before bedtime so all family members are not overstimulated and are calm and ready for bedtime.

## Summary

We can summarize:

1.   Cyclothymic disorder, bipolar spectrum disorders have been linked to bulimia nervosa and binge eating disorder, disturbed eating behaviors that cause health and mental health problems. By treating these mood disorders with counseling, medical intervention, psychopharmacology, we can manage mood changes that encourage eating disorders. And we can go on to encourage healthy nutrition through mentoring, education, classes, and small group participation. Young people need support as they learn to cope with eating disorders and challenges of making good choices in our complex world.

2.   Many youth and students consume high levels of carbohydrates, (pizzas, cereals, breads, donuts), gluten, and sugar daily. These poor eating practices lead to malnutrition where our children do not get the nutrients, vitamins, minerals, antioxidants, brain fat (DHA), they need to thrive, and grow healthy brains and healthy bodies. (Perlmutter, 2013, 2015)

3. The brain also can become inflamed due to overconsumption of gluten and due to 'gluten sensitivity'. It's hard to concentrate and study when your body feels ill and your head feels too warm or is dealing with a migraine. Perlmutter recommends taking probiotic and other supplements to calm and focus the mind. (Perlmutter, 2013).

4. Dr. Fife, Dr. Perlmutter and other physicians who have studied nutrition know that our brains and bodies need natural, organic fats in our diet to function and work well. Eggs, avocados, whole milk yogurt, virgin coconut oil and olive oil can provide the good fats our bodies need for energy and for helping our brain function well. Omega-3 fats, eating grain fed beef, lamb or pork or wild fish will provide the healthy fat and protein our brains and bodies need. Such nutrition encourages our body and gastrointestinal system to have a normal microbiome in the gut and to have normal excretion of foods consumed. When the body feels normal and calm, sleep can come naturally and so follows better mood states.

5. Fermented foods have had a long history as being a crucial part of healthy Korean, Japanese, European diets. These foods played an important nutritional role in preventing illness and promoting health in their families. Dr. Perlmutter outlined how to make these fermented foods and use them in your daily diet. It's easy to weave them in with your favorite meals. Greek yogurts, pickled beets, sauerkraut, kefir can be blended into your meals.

6. Dr. Bieler explained how important vegetables are not just for nutrition but also for cleansing toxins out of our endocrine organs and our body. *Food is Your Best_Medicine_*is a key reference for kidney and liver health. (Bieler, 1965)

7. Avoid eating carbohydrates, sugar, hydrogenated vegetable oil/foods. Move towards eating natural Omega-3 fat, protein foods and probiotics that promote calm gut and mind so that you and your student may have normal sleep patterns. Your mind will likely work better the next morning, the next day and for weeks to come.

# Chapter 8

# PMI: An Efficient Assessment Tool

---

**"Assessment before treatment saves time, saves dollars, and may save lives." Dr. John Paulus: 8/11/2016.**

Over the past 25 years parents, adults and teens reported that their doctors prescribed medications (antidepressants, psychostimulants, and sometimes neuroleptics/ anti-psychotic medication) to treat attention/deficit disorders, depression, paranoid thinking and to manage "anxiety". On occasion these patients reported that they received little benefit and little satisfaction from these prescribed medications. Several students and young adults expressed in frustration: "The medications don't seem to do anything." Or: "I just get an upset stomach from this medication."

It is important to use structured diagnostic interviews to evaluate depressive symptoms, to assess sleep behavior and patterns. Such interviews were used to evaluate a student's drinking and drug behavior. Often patients reported that their physicians did not have time to do a thorough evaluation. They were fortunate to talk with their doctor for 10 minutes. Several patients and students expressed anxiety and fear of telling their doctors about medication side effects.

This psychologist encouraged them to Google their medications and print-out side effects. He instructed them to use a colored marker to mark and underline any side effects they experienced. Then they were able to confidently share their page with the treating psychiatrist, doctor, or nurse. College students sometimes reported having problems going to sleep and remaining asleep. At such times we completed a psychiatric sleep inventory from a New York practice. When this sleep-waking data was included with my reports, my diagnoses and conclusions became more comprehensive and understandable.

Some parents and students commented: "You are the first doctor or psychologist to tell me that I may not have ADHD, and may have a mood disorder, or a sleep disorder. Many young adults expressed relief at finally getting an answer, a direction, or an alternative diagnosis for treatment. "That ADHD medication just wasn't helping me. I continued to be distractible, grouchy, or angry with my parents, my friends" were words I often heard.

In late 1990's, this provider had practiced psychological treatment with families for seven years. Although this psychologist was well versed in ADHD evaluations and testing, he ran across some students with mood symptoms and sleep problems which had a negative effect on their schoolwork and peer relationships. This mental health provider needed a tool to administer to parents that would give me a clear picture of what was contributing to school and interpersonal problems.

This psychologist created a psychological tool to help me in my practice. This mental health provider called it the PMI, short for the Paulus Mood Inventory. When this provider developed this mood inventory it was used weekly in my private practice. When this psychologist left my private practice, he took this inventory to my university psychology practice and used it with families there.

This inventory bridged the divide between ADHD disorders and mixed mood disorders with related disruptive behavior, sleep, and appetite problems. At the time, this mental health practitioner was unaware of any psychological inventory that evaluated Cyclothymic disorders in teenagers and pre-adolescent youth. He took what he knew of how Cyclothymic disorders affected students in school, with peers, and at home, and worked those behavioral signs and symptoms into this rating scale.

To make this inventory effective, this evaluator needed enough mood symptoms, sleep and insomnia problems, behavioral problems, and items that describe problems with thinking, concentration, and distractibility. All these items related to mood and sleep disorders, and sometimes these behaviors related to attention disorders or other neurological problems.

This psychologist constructed a 70- item inventory that parents could rate the student on a Likert scale of 0, 1, or 2. When an item is rated a 2, it meant that it was a problem most of the time. A rating of 1 meant that this item was a problem some of the time, and a rating of 0 meant that this item was not a concern. The following items are 70 signs and symptoms of a Cyclothymic Disorder listed on the PMI inventory. This assessment tool needs to be standardized through a research study across several universities in the coming years.

## PMI

Name:_____ Age:_____ DOB: _____ Sex:_____

Grade in School:_____ Parent's Name: _____Date: _____

Directions: Listed below are symptoms or behaviors that describe young persons. For each item that describes your child now or in the past 6 months, circle the number that best describes your child. Circle 0 if it is not true; circle 1 if it is sometimes true for your child; and circle 2 if it is often true or very true.

|  | Not true | Sometimes true | Often true |
|---|---|---|---|
| 1. Needs to be continually doing something | 0 | 1 | 2 |
| 2. Has trouble concentrating | 0 | 1 | 2 |
| 3. Bossy; wants to run things. | 0 | 1 | 2 |
| 4. Stays close to adults | 0 | 1 | 2 |
| 5. Chews on clothes, other items | 0 | 1 | 2 |
| 6. Nervous or uncomfortable with groups | 0 | 1 | 2 |
| 7. Lacks judgment; gets in trouble | 0 | 1 | 2 |
| 8. Sensitive to what others say | 0 | 1 | 2 |
| 9. Complains of headaches | 0 | 1 | 2 |
| 10. Sleeps during the day; sometimes at school | 0 | 1 | 2 |
| 11. Shy or quiet with others | 0 | 1 | 2 |
| 12. Screams; gets or talks loud | 0 | 1 | 2 |

| | | | |
|---|---|---|---|
| 13. Jumps from one thing to another quickly | 0 | 1 | 2 |
| 14. Bullies; may be mean to others | 0 | 1 | 2 |
| 15. Eats too little or too much | 0 | 1 | 2 |
| 16. Unable to relax | 0 | 1 | 2 |
| 17. Things have to be perfect, specific way | 0 | 1 | 2 |
| 18. Has nightmares; wakes up a lot | 0 | 1 | 2 |
| 19. Early riser; ready to go in morning | 0 | 1 | 2 |
| 20. Can't wait; impatient | 0 | 1 | 2 |
| 21. Sulks, pouts, seems unhappy | 0 | 1 | 2 |
| 22. Complains of being hot | 0 | 1 | 2 |
| 23. Punches people or walls | 0 | 1 | 2 |
| 24. Serious; worries about adult things | 0 | 1 | 2 |
| 25. Destroys things, clothing | 0 | 1 | 2 |
| 26. Secretive, keeps things to self | 0 | 1 | 2 |
| 27. Feels others can't be trusted | 0 | 1 | 2 |
| 28. Often talks about his/her size | 0 | 1 | 2 |
| 29. Talks about death or dying | 0 | 1 | 2 |
| 30. Easily sidetracked; mind moves quickly | 0 | 1 | 2 |
| 31. Bites fingernails | 0 | 1 | 2 |
| 32. Plays with own sex parts | 0 | 1 | 2 |
| 33. Whines a lot or complains | 0 | 1 | 2 |
| 34. Demanding; constantly at your elbow | 0 | 1 | 2 |
| 35. Wets self or the bed | 0 | 1 | 2 |
| 36. Hits, kicks or slaps others | 0 | 1 | 2 |
| 37. Has a short temper, gets annoyed easily | 0 | 1 | 2 |
| 38. Butts into conversations, interrupts | 0 | 1 | 2 |
| 39. Laughs loud and talks loudly | 0 | 1 | 2 |
| 40. "Know-it-all"; can't be told | 0 | 1 | 2 |
| 41. Energetic, speedy. | 0 | 1 | 2 |
| 42. Doesn't listen | 0 | 1 | 2 |
| 43. Very active, seems hyperactive | 0 | 1 | 2 |
| 44. Little or no interest/ after school activities | 0 | 1 | 2 |
| 45. Talks in sleep; tosses and turns in sleep | 0 | 1 | 2 |
| 46. Argues; gets jealous | 0 | 1 | 2 |
| 47. Possessive of belongings | 0 | 1 | 2 |

| | 0 | 1 | 2 |
|---|---|---|---|
| 48. Fidgets with things frequently | 0 | 1 | 2 |
| 49. Complains of being tired or bored | 0 | 1 | 2 |
| 50. Dislikes school or doesn't want to go | 0 | 1 | 2 |
| 51. Has hurt or cut self | 0 | 1 | 2 |
| 52. Gets into fights; loses self-control | 0 | 1 | 2 |
| 53. Does poor school work, careless | 0 | 1 | 2 |
| 54. Everything has to be a certain way | 0 | 1 | 2 |
| 55. Talks fast or too much | 0 | 1 | 2 |
| 56. Bad behavior at school | 0 | 1 | 2 |
| 57. Has sudden changes in mood | 0 | 1 | 2 |
| 58. Gets angry easily | 0 | 1 | 2 |
| 59. Gets stubborn or irritable | 0 | 1 | 2 |
| 60. Impulsive or disappears quickly | 0 | 1 | 2 |
| 61. Has crying spells | 0 | 1 | 2 |
| 62. Disobeys or refuses to do as asked | 0 | 1 | 2 |
| 63. Curses or yells at others | 0 | 1 | 2 |
| 64. Goes from irritable to avoiding others | 0 | 1 | 2 |
| 65. Has few or no friends | 0 | 1 | 2 |
| 66. Anxious or nervous | 0 | 1 | 2 |
| 67. Dislikes school, doesn't want to go | 0 | 1 | 2 |
| 68. Has trouble sleeping at night | 0 | 1 | 2 |
| 69. Impulsive, moves on quickly | 0 | 1 | 2 |
| 70. Trouble winding down in evening | 0 | 1 | 2 |

Please share anything else that concerns you about your daughter or son's sleep, behavior, schoolwork, relating to others, and her/his treatment of animals.

_____

_____

_____

_____

Note: This PMI inventory had been used since the late 1990's in my psychology practice as an experimental tool. Average total score on the PMI (n = 25) for 25 students seen from July 1997 to February 2000 for ages 4 to 18 is 61. The average score for the 30 item Mania scale for this group was 28.7. A score of 60 or above is significant for a Cyclothymic disorder. A score of 80 or higher may indicate a bipolar spectrum disorder or bipolar disorder. This PMI was often used with the *Millon Adolescent Clinical Inventory*, depression inventories, and behavior checklists to complete my data collection. Careful interviews with parents and caretakers that review medical history, family history, developmental history, and the child or teen's school history is essential to complete assessment of the student.

**Note**: All names of students and their parents have been changed to safekeep the identities of individual patients and their families.

### Case Example: The Moody Middle Schooler

The PMI proved to be useful in evaluating a 12- year-old student with multiple mental health problems. Michael reported a variety of problems including feeling depressed and sad, getting upset, having stomach aches, and he reported that two peers at school were mean to him. His mother reported that he had problems with distractibility, anxiety, concentration, and agitation. She stated that he was fearful, cried often, and felt hopeless. She reported her son had mood swings, made suicidal and homicidal statements, and was restless and demanding. This 12-year-old had angry, irritable, anxious, and depressed moods.

### Sleep problems

Michael's mother reported that he had insomnia, nightmares, and had a hard time going to sleep. Michael had erratic sleep patterns ranging from 4 to 8 hours of sleep per night. He had such sleep problems for several years.

The PMI is best used as part of a battery of psychological tests and inventories. Michael's parents completed the *Conners' Rating Scales (CPRS-48)*. Results indicated severe Conduct Problems, Learning Problems, Psychosomatic (health concern) Problems, Impulsive-Hyperactive behavior, and Hyperactivity.

The *Millon Pre-Adolescent Clinical Inventory (M-PACI)* is a brief personality inventory. Michael completed this inventory in a straightforward, honest manner. *M-PACI* results indicated a Personality pattern of significant Unruly traits and Confident, Outgoing, and Unstable personality features and behaviors.

He was administered the *Conners' Continuous Performance Test II (CPT-II)* to determine the possible effect of his ADHD disorder and medication on his vigilance, attention, and impulsivity. With the assistance of Adderal and an anticonvulsant medication, Michael obtained a non-clinical profile for ADHD and attention problems. This computer test suggested he did not have ADHD. However, he did show impulsivity by making 27 Commission errors, when he pressed the mouse for the X letter when he should not have done so.

Michael's parents completed the PMI and Michael obtained a <u>high score of 105</u> indicating that he had a severe mood disorder, a Cyclothymic Disorder or manic- depressive illness. He was described as an angry, aggressive, moody, tense, highly impulsive child who was also seen as a sensitive, nervous, hyperactive, energetic child. A score above 100 meant that Michael had 30 or more depressive and hypomanic mood symptoms, and he had sleep and behavioral *problems most of the time*. He had 35 other signs or symptoms of emotional disturbance some of the time. A score of 60 to 74 indicated a moderate mood problem.

These results suggested that this young man *needed a comprehensive treatment* plan with treatment providers, including a psychiatrist and a psychologist familiar with treating mood disorders and trauma. It would be advisable for him to participate in group therapy for teaching social skills and problem solving, and to work with a play therapist to help resolve emotional, subconscious conflict. His family was referred to community groups to give Michael an opportunity to participate in scouting, youth fellowship, or to have a Big brother. Michael and his parents were referred for medical and mental health treatment of his mood disorder.

## Ideas to Improve Assessment

It is prudent to administer the PMI to parents separately as each parent will observe or see different behaviors, signs, and symptoms of Cyclothymic mood at differing times. When parents work different shifts, they will have day, evening, and nighttime observations of their teen or child for which the other may not have had the opportunity to witness.

Likewise, it is helpful to have the teenager to complete self-reports (like the *Youth Self-Report of the CBCL 4-18*) to provide more information on school and home behavior. The *Millon Clinical Inventories (MACI, M-PACI)* provide useful, supportive information on the personality and psychological functioning of adolescents and children respectively.

Several more examples of the PMI with teenagers and with children indicate that reliance on the *total score* of this inventory may be misleading. Some parents are hesitant to put their son or daughter in too much negative light. They may avoid reporting symptoms or not rate the severity of behaviors for their child or teen. Parents naturally want their child not to be too ill or mentally off the mark. Therefore, it is important for the psychologist to be well informed about bipolar spectrum disorder in children and youth. The well-trained psychologist will know what symptoms to give extra consideration and weight when determining a diagnosis for his patient.

## Cases That Illustrate the Usefulness of the PMI

Andy, age 17, was brought for a psychological evaluation by his mother who commented: "You never know the mood he's going to be in." Andy obtained a total PMI score of 104 from his mother's rating. Andy had trouble concentrating, was bossy and sensitive and had headaches. He was easily sidetracked, bit his fingernails, laughed, and talked loudly, and had sudden changes of mood.

Psychological testing indicated that he needed medical evaluation and mental health treatment of his Cyclothymic Disorder or early onset bipolar spectrum disorder. His mother was honest and straightforward in her report which helped in diagnosing Andy. Andy and his mother were referred to a psychiatrist for medical evaluation and treatment. Additionally, this psychologist referred them to an experienced clinical psychologist near their home for counseling.

Mark, age 15, was referred for psychological evaluation by his mother who suffered from a serious mood disorder and related anxiety and nervousness. Her son stressed her a great deal. She reported that he was disruptive at school, very unmotivated to do schoolwork and acted oppositional at home. His mother stated that he lacked judgment, screamed, jumped from one thing to another quickly, and bullied others. His mother expressed concern that he destroyed things, had restless sleep, got angry easily, and had trouble sleeping at night.

These were some of Mark's frequent behaviors and signs of mood. His score of 81 reflected the severity of his problems. A score of 75 and above is in the severe range and indicated he had a "mood swing disorder". He likely had a Cyclothymic Disorder to go along with his Borderline intellectual functioning.

Mark and his mother were referred to his treating psychiatrist and a report was sent outlining his problems and treatment recommendations. Due to his parents' mental health and life problems, Mark was seen for treatment only occasionally and continued to have problems at school and elsewhere.

## A case of Hypomanic, energetic, angry mood warrants caution in medical treatment.

Sarah, age 15, and her mother presented a slightly different picture and constellation of concerns. Her mother, Diane, reported: "Last summer she was real revved up" and she had an episode of energetic (hypomanic) mood. As we reviewed the PMI results, her mother commented about Sarah getting angry easily: "She has a quick temper, an explosive temper a lot like her Dad." We examined her trouble sleeping at night, and Sarah reported that 'she is waking up a lot'.

Sarah had 17 symptoms of hypomanic mood including trouble concentrating, thoughts racing through her mind, aggressive behavior, and loud/excitable speech. She became angry easily and became irritable and impulsive. Her total score of 62 is in the Moderate range and indicated that she needed medical and mental health treatment for a Cyclothymic disorder. Antidepressant medication can encourage more hypomanic/ manic mood and behavior, therefore, parents and treatment providers need to take caution in what is prescribed. Medical treatment with anti-manic medicine, usually anti-convulsant medication, is recommended by medical researchers familiar with mood swing disorders.

### The Hypomanic Boy Who Could Not Sleep or Concentrate

Rebecca brought her son, Danny, age 7, to see me because he had a number of frequent behavioral, mood and sleep problems. She appreciated this inventory and commented that she underlined the items that most applied to her son. She marked 32 manic mood signs and symptoms and commented: "Danny has to be told to do something at least 2 or 3 times. He seems to be out in space almost all of the time."

Rebecca underlined or wrote that Danny wakes up at night, worries about adult things, interrupts his parents (and others), rolls around in his sleep, argues, complains of being bored, and worries too much. This bright lady and her bright son were able to report important psychological information.

Due to their accurate and honest reporting, Danny obtained a PMI total score of 90. Testing results and clinical interviews indicated the presence of a manic-depressive mood disorder or a Cyclothymic Disorder. Rebecca reported that her son's pediatrician started him on 125 mg. of a low dose of an anticonvulsant, mood stabilization medication, and Danny had a good response to this GABA medication.* He began to sleep better and became less worried.

(Note: Children under age 5 are not prescribed this medication because their livers are not developed or mature enough to manage this anticonvulsant. Liver function tests are needed to ascertain good liver functioning).

## Important to Use Caution and Low Doses with Medication

*Medications need to be used with great caution in children and teenagers. Most doctors, psychiatrists and pediatricians begin medications at low dosages to avoid causing any harm and to prevent side effects. For medical treatment of the Cyclothymic child, parents would be wise to consult Akiskal, H.S., Tohen, M., Editors, *Bipolar Psychopharmacotherapy: Caring for the Patient* in working with a treating child psychiatrist or nurse practitioner. (Akiskal, Tohen, 2011).

*Be aware that anticonvulsant medications are processed by the liver, liver function tests may be recommended, and blood levels need to be taken to determine therapeutic levels. Anticonvulsant medication is not prescribed to patients four or younger due to immature liver development. Young children cannot eliminate or discharge this medication properly, and it could damage their livers or cause toxicity.

Preston, O'Neal, and Talaga (2015) provide a thorough discussion in the medical treatment of bipolar disorders, depression and anxiety disorders in their excellent text: *Child and Adolescent Clinical Psychopharmacology Made Simple, third edition.* Their chapter 3 describes manic-depressive illness or bipolar disorder in detail, differentiates bipolar disorder from ADHD, and details medical treatment. Chapter 8 of their text has helpful information on Sleep Disorders, treating Conduct disorders, and an instructive section on Substance Use.

## Even a Low Score on the PMI with Other Data Provides Direction for Treatment

Linda, age 12, came in with her parents who were concerned about her mood and her sleep patterns. Linda's parents commented that she "gets goofy and silly" and "she gets very energetic at night." Her parents described her mood and behavior in the following words: "She's bossy, sensitive, shy or quiet with others, and she sulks, pouts or seems unhappy". They added (on the PMI) that she is secretive, can be an early riser, is easily sidetracked, is energetic at night, and does not listen. Linda complains of being bored, does poorly in school, gets angry easily and irritable, curses or yells, argues, and has stomach aches.

Linda is nervous and uncomfortable with groups. Noise and over-stimulation is a big problem for students with Cyclothymic disorder.

Linda obtained a score of 51 on the PMI and her total score along with clinical information and interviews, was enough to indicate a presence of a mood/sleep disorder. Significant energetic, restless, nervous, hypomanic mood is present. Linda and her parents were referred to a treating psychiatrist to further evaluate her mood and sleep disorders.

**Summary**:

The PMI inventory of 70 mood and behavior items may be one useful tool in gathering data or information on children, students, or teenagers to determine whether they have a mood disorder such as Dysthymia, Depressive mood, or a Cyclothymic disorder. While some of the items may describe an oppositional defiant disorder, a conduct disorder, an attention problem, sleep problems, or a possible anxiety disorder, together, these signs and symptoms likely point to a mood disorder.

It is important to take a careful educational, medical, family mental health history, and to use other psychological tests or assessments, in evaluating the student to arrive at an accurate and comprehensive diagnosis and treatment direction.

Chapter 9 examines suicidal depression. This next chapter explains how and why effective assessment of mood and sleep disorders is important in preventing suicide.

## Chapter 9

# Suicidal Depression and
# Effective Interventions

---

## Introduction

Rates of suicide have increased dramatically in the United States for children, teenagers, and young adults. Suicide is one of the leading causes of death for these young people. Like heart disease, suicide can be prevented. This chapter reviews data and research on suicide and what can be done to prevent this tragic, impulsive behavior. Suicidal behavior is often related to mood swing disorders and Cyclothymic disorder.

## Why I Wrote This Guide

Suicide is the leading cause of death among Ohio children ages 10 to 14, according to the Ohio Department of Health's report released November 2019. The Ohio Suicide Demographics and Trends Report for 2018 reported: "The number of suicides among preteens ages 10 to 14 increased by 56 percent from 2007 to 2018." "For Ohioans aged 15 to 34, suicide was the second leading cause of death."

Suicide rates and numbers are difficult to track and calculate. Some suicides may be completed in a covert manner such as a car accident, an accidental fall, overdose on medication or an illegal drug, or accidental shooting of self. Numbers of suicides may be undercounted, underreported, and some parents or family members prefer not to report such behavior. * (In this chapter names have been changed to protect the identity of individuals and families).

Recent suicides of a 10-year-old boy and another 12-year-old boy in Ohio between 2018 and 2019 spurred me to write this guide. Somehow our culture and society in Ohio needs to find ways to prevent this behavior. We need to have supportive, trained people and peers in place to help locate these depressed and stressed-out children and encourage them towards healthy coping behavior. We need to encourage these students to seek help and support for their emotional distress and mood swings.

Cyclothymic Disorder, a mild to moderate manic-depressive illness, may be linked to severe episodes of depression and suicidal thinking. See oncoming studies in this chapter. Over the past twenty years, some of my mood disordered clients reported that they had thoughts of suicide as young as age 6. Such suicidal thinking is not uncommon in children between the ages of 7 and 12.

When elementary school age children face sufficient stress, they may feel helpless, vulnerable, and hopeless. When mood disordered students lack supportive adults in their lives, experience physical, emotional, and sexual abuse, or experience neglect with mood and personality disordered parents, they may become self-destructive *and have suicidal feelings and thoughts*.

## A Case Example of a Boy with Suicidal Thinking

Richard, age 11, is an example of a mood disordered young man who struggled with depressive thinking. He performed poorly with his schoolwork and was failing school. He had behavioral problems including stealing and setting fire to his bedroom carpet. Such behavior often is related to emotionally disturbed and mood disordered children. His physician and his county board of Developmental Disabilities requested psychological evaluation and testing. His doctor diagnosed him with ADHD and prescribed Adderall to control his hyperactive symptoms. Yet, his teacher did not see his attention span change nor improve.

We administered a comprehensive set of psychological tests, inventories, and behavioral checklists. WISC-IV Intelligence testing results were interesting with test scores ranging from a low scaled score of 1 on Digit

Span, suggesting a *distractible* mind, to Average scaled scores of 9 on Coding and Symbol Search. He performed better on these visual motor tasks of copying and locating symbols that required attention to detail. He performed low average on Block Design with a score of 8, a task of non-verbal reasoning.

His WISC-IV testing results are typical for a Cyclothymic, mood disordered middle school youth. These restless, distractible, and sometimes impatient students find it difficult to focus on verbal tests and questions when their minds are thinking of other tasks or are busy looking ahead. Yet, with hands-on tasks they can perform near the average range. Richard hummed while working on the Block Design test. This behavior may have been a sign that he liked this task. He rotated blocks quickly which caused mistakes and slowed his timed performance. Richard's nails were well chewed suggesting he may suffer with nervous mood.

His mother reported that he associated with older males and lacked friends at school. Richard completed *the Children's Depression Inventory* and marked several items that are typical of a depressed Cyclothymic youth. He reported that he was sad sometimes, behaved badly on occasion, and worried that bad things would happen to him. He marked the statements: 'I hate myself', and *"I think about killing myself but I would not do it."* He reported a need to push himself all the time to do 'my schoolwork'. He had many nights where he had trouble sleeping.

Evaluation results indicated that he was a moderately depressed, frustrated, restless person who was unhappy with himself and his place in the world. His treatment team, (parent, physicians, and therapist), *need to evaluate his suicidal ideation* on a regular basis as he proceeds through treatment. As he grows up his life's frustrations, stressors, and setbacks may mount up in the coming years.

His mother completed the *Child Symptom Inventory-4* and the PMI. She marked that he had impulsive, restless behavior, and had ADHD and hypomanic mood symptoms. These symptoms and behaviors included being unable to give close attention to details, not listening, and failing to finish things. He has difficulty organizing tasks, is easily distracted, is unable to stay seated, and talks excessively.

His mother described him as often blaming others, arguing with adults, and refusing to do as told. She reported that he is "often tense and unable to relax" and "he acts restless or edgy". Many of these signs and symptoms are typical of a hypomanic, Cyclothymic child.

The PMI (Paulus Mood Inventory) was described in detail in Chapter 8. The PMI results for Richard included a total score of 62. He had 43 signs and symptoms of restless, nervous, angry, tense, hypomanic and depressed mood. He had related behavioral and sleep problems. It is likely that Richard has a Cyclothymic Disorder or moderate manic - depression. This developmentally delayed middle school youth may be at risk for alcohol and/or drug abuse, impulsive behavior, antisocial behavior problems, and suicide in coming months.

His community, his school, and his treatment team need to keep a close watch on him and guide him through the treacherous shoals of his teenage years. Richard was referred to a child psychiatrist at a nearby hospital for ongoing treatment.

**To summarize:**

Richard age 11, a likely Cyclothymic mood disordered child has the following challenges:

1.  He has a medical mood swing disorder: Cyclothymic Disorder.
2.  He has developmental and intellectual delays.
3.  He has a behavioral disorder including fire setting which is a *common* coexisting behavior for bipolar spectrum children.
4.  He has a restless, distractible mind and restless, impulsive behavior often related to hypomanic mood. He feels nervous naturally.
5.  He has self-worth and self-hatred problems and suicidal ideation.
6.  His medical providers, parents and teachers are unaware of the severity of his mood disorder and believe he has ADHD.

Several of my Cyclothymic clients and bipolar patients reported that they began hurting themselves during elementary and middle school. This behavior often involved: cutting themselves, pulling out hair/ nails, chewing on fingernails or hitting their fists into walls and trees. These young people vented their emotional pain and frustration while exhibiting restless, energetic, overwhelmed minds and mood. These patients are sensitive individuals who have wired minds and hypomanic mood. They needed ways to calm and soothe themselves. *They needed mental health and medical treatment.*

## Little research exists on the presence of cyclothymic disorder and suicidal behavior.

In their research Tomba E., et al., found that *Cyclothymic patients obtained significantly higher scores* on depressed mood, pessimism, energy (level), phobic anxiety, avoidance, somatic anxiety, irritability, initial insomnia, and reactivity to social environment. (Tomba et al., 2012.)

## Cyclothymic disorder and suicidal behaviors:

Tomba et al., reviewed clinical information from mood and anxiety disorders regarding suicidal behavior and they concluded: "There is a particular cooccurrence of the wide range of cyclothymic features and suicide attempts and *the presence of cyclothymic disorders markedly increased the risk* of suicidal behavior." Children with cyclothymic mood disorders have rapid and frequent mood swings from hypomanic, irritable mood to withdrawn, depressed mood. (Tomba et al., 2012)

Perugi et al., completed an extensive review of data on mood disordered subjects with addictive and impulsive disorders and found that between 20% to 50% of them were affected by cyclothymia. They found that "cyclothymia was linked to a high risk of impulsive and suicidal behavior." *Perugi et al (2015): 119.*

In other words, young people *with cyclothymic disorder* will show a changing array of behaviors and moods. They may be tearful at times, happy or jocular, depressed, irritable, nervous, impulsive, or avoidant around others. These shifting moods may make these young people <u>more vulnerable</u> to suicidal ideation and behavior, and the abuse of alcohol and drugs.

## National Conference on Suicide and Causes of Death

On March 28, 2014 this psychologist had the privilege to travel to Houston to attend *The Problem of Suicide: Rediscovering Hope, The First John M. Oldham National Mental Health Symposium.* One learning objective was to teach participants to be able to recommend preventive public health interventions shown to be effective in reducing deaths by suicide.

John F. Greden, M.D. from the University of Michigan presented "Suicide Epidemiology, the Lack of Progress" in suicide prevention. He reported that in the United States suicide is one of the top <u>three causes</u> of death among ages 15 -24. Suicide is the 2nd cause of death in college students. He reported that suicide is the 1st cause of death among medical students.

## Assessment of Suicidal Risk

Dr. Greden discussed variables that may predict suicide and listed the following Risk Variables: Depressions and bipolar illnesses, substance abuse, guns, discharge from hospital (including ER) and contagion. When a friend or a relative commits suicide, the child or teen may find this life/death decision to be contagious. He instructed <u>us *to avoid*</u> the use of fad words such as 'copycat' suicide, 'successful suicide', and other words implying stereotypical behavior and thoughtless action. Dr. Greden expressed a dislike of glib assumptions about suicidal behavior.

Dr. Greden explained lack of progress in preventing suicide. He reported that the *inadequate diagnosis and treatment of depressions and bipolar illnesses is a major underlying variable* preventing progress in the treatment of suicidal depression. Let me repeat, he stated that the inadequate diagnosis and treatment of mood disorders is a major reason in preventing progress in treatment of suicidal depression /manic depression. He recommended the use of C-SSRS (Columbia Suicide Severity Rating Scale) in assessment and prevention of suicidal behavior.

Maria A. Oquendo, M.D. from the Department of Psychiatry of Columbia University spoke regarding *The Neurobiology of Suicide* on March 28, 2014 at the Problem of Suicide symposium. She proposed the presence of aggression, impulsivity, severe personality disorders, substance abuse disorders, family history of suicidal acts and physical illness contributed to possible suicidal behavior. She cited acute intoxication and *mood instability* as potential factors in suicidal behavior. Dr. Oquendo linked childhood adversity and hardship experiences with suicidal behavior. She stated that childhood traumatic experiences seem to be associated with later depression, impulsivity, and suicidal acts.

Stanley and Barter completed a study of adolescent suicide attempters at the University of Colorado Medical Center, Denver, Colorado. These medical doctors found that: The pre-hospital biography of suicide attempters differs significantly in two characteristics: "(1) a greater incidence of parent loss before age 12, and (2) more frequent threatened parent loss through talk of divorce or separation." Stanley and Barter (1970): p.91.

Brent et al completed at study of 63 adolescent suicide victims and found that victims were more likely to have had major depression, substance abuse, a past suicide attempt, family history of depression, treatment with tricyclic antidepressant, history of legal problems, and a handgun available in the home. Brent et al, (1994): pp. 193-202. It is worthwhile to examine the work of Berman & Jobes (2005, 1992) for a broader discussion of the assessment of youth suicide.

Baiden et al., investigated the relationship between age of first use of alcohol and suicidal ideation in high school students. Using a sample of 10,745 adolescents, they found suicidal ideation with 1801 adolescents. Some 1681 adolescents first used alcohol before age 13. These researchers found that alcohol use before age 13 was related to increased suicidal ideation among adolescents. (Baiden et al., 2019).

**Diagnostic Challenges with Mixed Mood States and Suicidal Risk**

Algorta et al., found that mixed mood features explain why bipolar disorder is associated both with a high rate of suicide attempts and a high rate of suicide completions. These authors found: "youth suicidality was significantly related to poor family functioning, low youth QoL (quality of life), and mixed mood features" with these pediatric bipolar youth. *Algorta et al, (2011):* p.82.

Van Meter A. et al described the challenges in diagnosing and treating Cyclothymic disorder. They stated that individuals with cyclothymic disorder often do not seek treatment for their mood disturbance. These individuals lack insight that their experience is dysfunctional, particularly during periods of elevated mood. And mood symptoms may not be severe enough to encourage action by treatment providers or family, such as hospitalization or arrest. Van Meter et al (2012)

Van Meter et al. discussed the problems of misdiagnosis. These researchers stated if the clinician and the patient do not fully comprehend the episodic nature of cyclothymic disorder: (the mood changes), "the person may be misdiagnosed with a personality disorder, oppositional defiant disorder, or ADHD". It is easy to confuse mixed moods with such diagnoses. As a result, prompt treatment of a cyclothymic disorder is prevented. (Van Meter et al, 2012): 235. Fields, Fristad, 2009, and Youngstrom, 2009 found similar problems with misdiagnosis.

Perugi etal., 2015 described the connection between cyclothymic disorder in patients and the risk of suicide. "The frequent presence of mixed features and impulsivity during depressive phases makes cyclothymic patients more likely to act on suicidal impulses". Papolos and Papolos stated that the greatest risk for suicide occurs when a child is in a mixed mood state. The child in this mood state "experiences a combination of the terrible feelings of depression with the frenzied agitation and energy of mania." Such mood states can be induced by the use of antidepressant medication. (Papolos and Papolos, 1999): 234.

Multiple research studies on major depression and suicide have found that cyclothymic temperament is linked to significantly higher numbers of past suicide attempts. (Akiskal etal., 2006a; Mechri etal., 2011). Rapid mood cycling further increases the risk of suicide (Azorin, etal., 2010). A.L. Berman discusses the issues and challenges in evaluating adolescent suicide Berman, 1986a.

## Suicide-specific interventions:

Thomas E. Ellis, PsyD. from the Baylor College of Medicine, shared interventions that may be *helpful in preventing suicide*. He made the following recommendations: frequent suicide-specific assessment, addressing the "drivers" of suicidality, written safety plans, restriction of means to commit suicide and problem-solving training. He recommended the use of the following in treatment: coping cards, Hope box, reasons for living/dying, distress tolerance training, imaginal rehearsal, and participating in a suicide resilience group.

Suicide prevention in schools and suicide interventions was examined thirty years ago (Berman, 1990b). Yet it continues to be an area of increasing concern as rates of suicide have increased during the last 20 years.

Shawn Shea, M.D. is the President/Director of the Training Institute for Suicide Assessment and Clinical Interviewing. He presented *The Practical Art of Suicide Assessment*. He invented the *Chronological Assessment of Suicide Events – CASE* approach. Dr. Shea recommended use of his *suicide assessment.com* website. He reported that 50% of persons who committed suicide *had seen* a physician, nurse, or physician assistant in the previous month. He saw the need to train nurses and doctors to ask sophisticated questions. He believed that teaching them to be competent and comfortable in asking the right questions in sufficient depth could help prevent suicide.

In *Chronological Assessment of Suicide Events*, Dr. Shea examines past events of the following: suicidal behavior and thinking including recent events (in the last 2 months), presenting events, and immediate events. A behavioral incident is explored by asking a question about a specific act or thought (fact-finding behavioral incident). For example: "Did you make the rope into a noose?" Or asking what happened next (sequencing behavioral incident) as with: "What did you do next?"

Dr. Shea uses 'gentle assumption' as a validity technique to explore deeper into suicidal behavior and thinking. This technique is used when a clinician suspects that a patient will be hesitant to discuss a taboo topic. The clinician assumes that the potentially embarrassing behavior occurs and frames the question accordingly, in a gentle tone of voice. Example: "What other ways have you thought of killing yourself?" Or: "What other drugs have you used in the past two weeks?"

**Supportive Family Encourages Resiliency and May Prevent Suicide**

Some of the research studies in this chapter underlined the importance of supportive family environments. Past research has indicated what a crucial role parents play in nurturing and encouraging success in school, and in social activities and sports. Werner and Smith, 1982 described how parents may encourage resiliency in their children and youth as they face both external and internal (mood, anxiety, nervousness) stressors. Resilient youth have encouraging mentors who may be a caring aunt, an interested uncle, a nurturing grandparent, stepparent, or parent. These adults mentor youth in coping well with stress. Werner and Smith, (1982).

**Case example: Sam, Suicidal Teenager**

One tragic youth who committed suicide had many of the ingredients that are described in this chapter, in his life. This teen came from a single parent home and lived with his mother. The young man struggled with school, and he received no encouragement from his alcohol prone father, who never showed up when needed. His mother suffered from severe bouts of depression and had a history of mood changes. She sought treatment for her mood disorder and was encouraging and supportive of her son and his counseling.

Sam's mother encouraged him to seek help for his behavioral, attention, distractibility problems. He received some counseling at his school. His counselor diagnosed the young man as having ADHD. He was treated with ADHD medication (an antidepressant) in addition to therapy at a clinic. He soon lost motivation for therapy and instead pursued his favorite sport. After he graduated from high school, his mother left for a brief vacation. His father failed to show up to give him a ride to his sport event. Tragically, a friend who was busy working, could not leave to pick him up.

Sam, age 17, became agitated, frustrated, and upset. He picked up an available family handgun and shot himself. As Sam did not receive the *adequate* treatment needed for his mood disorder, nor did he obtain the support from his father, he was at a high risk of suicide.

As Stanley and Barter, 1970 and Algorta et al.,2012 reported, parental conflict and lack of emotional support by a parent plays a big role in suicide of psychiatric patient, or cyclothymic and bipolar youth. Sam's parents had chronic conflict over father's lack of emotional support of Sam. Both parents had serious mood disorders, which contributed to arguments and conflict, and his father abused substances which made responsible parenting difficult.

It may be that the three factors Algorta et al., 2012 described: mixed mood symptoms, family functioning, and QoL (quality of life) played a significant role in Sam's suicide. Possible mixed mood symptoms and mood swings, and the availability of a handgun in the home, contributed to his suicidal act.

**Summary:**

Suicidal behavior in children and teenagers is a complex subject with a multitude of possible causes. Remember that depression and bipolar spectrum disorders may be one important influence in this behavior. Environmental, family, and personal stressors may play an important role in suicide. Lack of parental and family support is a vulnerability factor in suicidal behavior.

However, resilience or doing well in coping with stressors was found to be linked to having a key adult family member being a good mentor providing emotional support for achievement and vocational skills training. (Werner E., Smith, R., 1982).

Let's summarize this rather complex subject of suicide during childhood and adolescence from research presented in this chapter:

1. Loss of one or more parents or parental divorce is a risk factor in suicide of children and teens when they have a mood disorder and lack of support.

2. When a child or adolescent has a Cyclothymic Disorder or a bipolar spectrum disorder, has mood swings, lacks supervision, and has the means to commit suicide, he or she may be at high risk of suicide.

3. Alcohol and drug use, particularly when begun before the age of 13, places mood disordered teenagers at risk for suicidal behavior.

4. Poor family functioning, family discord / conflict, and lack of support and encouragement of the child to learn and to acquire educational and work skills, is a risk factor for suicidal behavior and depression.

5. A poor quality of life that lacks money, time, and encouragement for learning reading, writing, math skills, for strategic game skills, test-taking skills, and for travel to museums and to other countries and cities, places children and teenagers at a great disadvantage to students whose parents provide these opportunities. This lack of quality of life (QoL) pulls down mood and motivation for many children and adolescents.

6. This chapter reported that mood swings, mood instability and mixed mood presentations present a risk of suicide to children. Therefore, good psychological and psychiatric assessment and treatment are needed to head off suicidal behavior.

7. Mood stability, good sleep patterns, a healthy nutrition plan, exercise with family and friends, and a good support group at school or church, temple, or mosque fortifies young people with energy, inspiration, and may help prevent suicidal behavior.

Suicide prevention groups and task forces are needed at state, community levels. We need such groups in community centers and libraries, and at schools and churches. These groups need to include adults, adolescents, and children.

## Chapter 10

# Comprehensive Treatment
# of Cyclothymic Disorder

While working in private practice of psychology this provider enjoyed the opportunity to work with several children and families who were referred for psychological evaluation and treatment by the county children services. As this psychologist worked with mood disordered parents who were anxious and had several health and somatic complaints, this mental health practitioner saw that their children had many of the same symptoms. A number of these children were high-strung, hyperactive, and restless. With mood disordered children, traditional talk therapy is often not possible without adding hands-on activities.

Over the years, this psychologist found that he could best engage children and pre-teens in therapy with such activities as drawing, coloring pictures, playing The Feelings Wheel Game, and talking while they were channeling their energy through multiple tasks. These restless, anxious and sometimes temperamental students began to relax and enjoy therapy while learning new games, words, and strategies.

Therefore, with the use of drawing, sand tray, clay work, and therapeutic games, we calmed them and built rapport. They were very motivated to return for family therapy. Child play therapy was rewarding, non-punitive, safe, and accepting. These children began to feel more positive about themselves.

## The Magic of Play Therapy in Building Rapport

Violet Oaklander reported in **Windows to Our Children** that play therapy is a good medium for children to express their feelings and struggles. Like her, this practitioner found that nervous, restless children enjoyed hands-on activities and were more able to talk and be engaged in therapy. In play and child therapy, we used clay and Playdoh to make characters for our pretend play. The use of a sand tray and plastic animals, people, and soldiers was enjoyable and relaxing for children. We constructed small ponds for animals, made roads, hills, and grazing areas for animals. Play therapy helped to manage anxious, nervous mood and the hesitation to talk.

(Oaklander, 1998).

Some years ago, this mental health provider had a young man in for the first time, and he was immediately drawn to my Lego set. There were two dragons with red wings and black wings, respectively, the witch, the wagons and horses and some soldiers. At one point the dragons were fighting each other. "What do they say?" This therapist queried. "Give the dragons a voice." He answered: "I'm going to win. I'm going to be the boss." This second grader came from a home where his Dad was very impatient and sometimes short-tempered. Jonny gave me some clues as to his emotional needs. This student would like to have a greater sense of being in emotional control. We could now explore this issue further in therapy and treatment.

### A case example of a Cyclothymic teenager and use of drawing.

Barry, a 15-year-old had increasing academic and interpersonal problems. He recently expressed a desire to hit his teacher and hurt peers who were teasing him. This young man showed many symptoms of a cyclothymic disorder including anger outbursts, being argumentative with his mother and others, inability to focus, sleep problems, and mood changes.

We decide to try out some of the drawing/visual imagery techniques suggested by Violet Oaklander (1998) with this rather quiet, withdrawn individual. He drew a picture of a small boat in a storm. "How does the boat feel?"

Barry: "He's scared. "Tired". "The boat's trying to get through the storm and it is hitting the waves; and back there it's real calm."

"How is this like your life?"

"There are times of smooth sailing and rough times."

"Any other ways?"

"Of tempers (he and his mother). Sometimes we're calm and sometimes raging mad."

We go on to have Barry visualize he is a spider building a web in the rain. This session was the most fruitful of several sessions. We proceeded to work closely with a psychiatrist to treat his mood disorder while we continue our counseling.

## Additional Activities to Engage Restless, Anxious Students in Therapy

Board games like the Talking, Doing and Feeling Game and The Coping Skills Game* with cards, dice, and play pieces, and Othello, a fast-moving strategy game, are motivating for Cyclothymic students. These activities give students increasing confidence in their abilities to read, count, think and play with another person.

These therapeutic games encourage positive thinking as the child or teen sees that they can learn to express feelings in a comfortable way, and do new activities rather quickly. They begin to think and feel: "I can count better than I thought." "My reading is improving the more I play this game." "I can manage my feelings, express my feelings and this therapist accepts my feelings." "It feels good to play in a safe environment and everyone feels like they are having fun and a good time." (See Reference section for information regarding these games).

When there are indications of physical, sexual abuse and neglect of a child, the treating psychologist or therapist is mandated by psychology law and ethics to report this harm to authorities, police, and/or a treating children's hospital center. By doing so, the psychologist or therapist prevents further harm of the child, possible suicide, and eventual development of a disturbed personality who seeks to harm, hurt, and sometimes kill others.

### How do I as a parent seek needed therapy and treatment for my mood, disordered child?

Step 1: Do some research. You can call your state psychological association to obtain a list of psychologists specializing in the treatment of children and teenagers. You can select those therapists experienced in working with children who have mood disorders including depression, bipolar disorder, or cyclothymic disorder. In our state you can Google information on the Ohio Psychological Association (OPA). You can also call your university for information and referrals to treatment providers. You can call your university child psychiatry department. In Columbus, Ohio, the Nationwide Children's Hospital has several children's clinics across the city.

Step 2: Once you speak to a psychologist, be sure to ask them about their experience and expertise in working with depressed, Cyclothymic depressed, and manic-depressive children and teens. They should be happy to share their experience with you. Be sure to ask them to describe to you how they plan to evaluate your son or daughter, what steps they would take, and assessment tools they plan to use.

Step 3: A competent psychologist knows that these mood disorders are complex and require a variety of tools, behavior checklists, inventories, and computer tests to fully diagnose them. Such a psychologist can describe the depression, anxiety, and mania inventories they use. They can describe the personality inventories they use to obtain a full picture of the mood symptoms, the anxiety, the stress, and the personality patterns of your young person. They may be able to do ADHD testing, memory testing and IQ testing to determine auditory and visual reasoning and memory strengths and weaknesses of your child or teen. Discuss with this treatment provider their plan of action for assessment and treatment.

By careful and thorough assessment, the psychologist can tell you what your son and daughters' strengths and vulnerabilities are. Is your daughter optimistic about school and her future? Does your son feel confident in his peer relations, in his schoolwork, and where he is going in his life? Are your son and daughter stressed, worried, sad, nervous, feeling pessimistic or even suicidal about their lives?

Step 4: This step 4 is most important in getting your daughter and son's problems resolved. After your psychologist compiles a psychological report of her/his findings, she/he **writes a referral letter and sends this report to the treating psychiatrist.** You may also want your family physician or pediatrician to refer your son or daughter to a treating psychiatrist when you talk with them, and they reviewed your psychologist's report.

Step 5: Ask your treating psychiatrist to explain his or her understanding of Cyclothymic disorder, how it is best evaluated. What are possible treatments? What treatments have they found to work well? They can share with you some of the latest research on treatment of this complicated mood disorder. Usually one medication may be needed to treat the depressive part or phase of the Cyclothymic disorders; and an anticonvulsant and/ or neuroleptic medication may be needed to manage hypomanic mood, paranoid /delusional thinking, rapid mood cycling, restless sleep and lack of restful sleep.

Step 6: Educate yourself on the medical treatments, medications, their interactions and side effects. Ask your daughter's and son's treating psychiatrist for information and resources on these medicines so you may read about them. Read some of the books listed in the References section and talked about in my chapters to better understand Cyclothymic disorder and its treatment. Talk to your pharmacist and have them print out information on medication and their interactions with other medications. They can give you the phone number of the company that manufactures the medication. Then you can talk to pharmacists at this company.

This mental health practitioner recommended reading *Hagop Akiskal and Mauricio Tohen, Editors,* (2011) regarding the medical treatment and psychopharmacotherapy of the bipolar spectrum/bipolar patient. Along with *D. Papolos and J. Papolos* (1999, 2002), guide on **The Bipolar Child**, you will have the expert references you need to help you understand the most appropriate medical treatment for your child or adolescent.

Wayne H. Green, M.D. (1991) in **Child and Adolescent Clinical Psychopharmacology** makes an important point about side effects of medications given to children: "The clinician must remember that the ability to understand (bad) <u>untoward</u> effects and verbalize unusual sensations, feelings, or discomfort not only varies among individual children but is developmentally determined." p.46. Younger children <u>report negative side effects</u> of medications <u>less frequently</u> than older children. The younger the child, the more urgent it is for caretakers to be actively looking for unwanted (side) effects.

It is necessary for the physician to ask the patient about side effects in language appropriate to the understanding of your child. (<u>untoward</u> = negative, uncomfortable, "unwanted" side effects). Be very careful in medicating young children as they may not be able to tell you or explain to you and the doctor the side effects they experience! This issue needs to be discussed with the treating physician or psychiatrist.

Step 7: Involve your active or moody child in group activities, particularly outdoor activities. Help your child choose activities to avoid crowds and noise that grate on the nerves of Cyclothymic teenagers and children. Scout troops, church youth fellowship groups of small size, arts and crafts activities, musical activities and theatre offer safe and supportive opportunities. With such activities your son or daughter can prosper with others and learn crucial pro-social skills.

Dr Perlmutter talks about the importance of exercise for brain functioning, for mental and physical health and for gut health. His book, **Brain Maker**, is a wonderful science book for the whole family and may encourage your student to pursue a career in health care. Be sure the whole family gets needed exercise daily of 30 minutes or more per day.

Step 8: Teenagers need purpose and direction. This psychologist recommends part time work and/or volunteer work activities for teenagers to encourage skills in working with others and for gaining confidence and mastery skills.

Step 9: Work with your therapist, school counselor, teacher, and other supportive adults to encourage your child or teen to communicate their feelings in safe, private ways. Your son or daughter can work out a private way of writing messages, letters, or sending drawings to caring, nurturing adults. In this way they let them know how they feel. For mood disordered young people, this step of sharing is very important to alleviating stress and finding timely help. It can make all the difference in the world.

Step 10: Celebrate your daughter's life and your son's life at different times of the year. Invite their friends and others to celebrate and hand out awards for "kind relationships", honesty, character, loyalty, "best friend to Ziggy" /her or his dog awards. Use humor, creativity, costumes, music, and food preparation. Let your daughter or son make a fun party with their friends (supervised by several supportive, caring parents). All kids have a need for recognition and positive experiences and memories.

**Frequent Parental Concerns**

**Anger**

Often parents tell me that their teen or child has a big problem with anger.

What can be done about it?

Parents have told me they have faced and dealt with their child's or teenager's anger and angry outbursts for months and even years. Most parents share that they have tried several ways of managing the young person's anger such as counseling and consequences at home or school. They report that their child has kicked or punched walls, hit or kicked other family members, threatened family members or teachers, and hit other students at school. These behaviors should not be ignored.

With the first phone call, this mental health provider suggests that the parent(s) come in for an 'overview' session to provide me background on their child and their developmental and behavioral history. The parent and he begin to investigate possible reasons for this anger and aggressive behavior. We begin to construct a treatment plan. We look at past explanations for angry or moody behavior and possible diagnostic impressions from teachers, therapists, and physician. What treatments have been tried? The parent is given a child behavior checklist to complete, and the child or teen's response to direction at home and school is described. Mood and sleep inventories help to describe problem behavior in detail.

We schedule an appointment for parent(s) and their teenager or child. We talk about how parents met and how each parent helped raise their child. When mother shared that father is currently in jail, the child or teen is asked when he last saw his father or talked to dad on the telephone or in person. We honestly and directly explore the current relationship of the child with his parents and the parents with each other. We avoid emotional games. We avoid 'Games People Play' (by Eric Berne). With child and family therapy honesty is the only policy. (Berne, 1967).

Often therapist gives the child or teen a task such as drawing a person, a house or a car. Sometimes they prefer drawing an animal, a monster, or a scene from a cartoon or video. Such activities are helpful for creating rapport, a positive atmosphere where praise can be given for their effort. It's a way of discharging restless energy. The parent or child are able to talk more effectively as everyone is in a positive, focused mood.

Possible problems such as past abuse or neglect, reactive attachment disorder when a child is adopted or neglected at an early age, or post-traumatic stress disorder are explored or ruled out as causes of current frustration, disappointment, and anger. Such topics are often discussed with the parent separately while the child is given another task.

The contribution of erratic sleep and sleep deprivation on anger and impatience and irritability is explained and explored. Parents and this therapist review the contribution of mood disorders such as Cyclothymic disorder with hypomanic mood, or early onset bipolar spectrum disorder, which can encourage, cause angry outbursts, mood swings, and lack of sleep or restless sleep.

**Specific Treatment for Anger and Mood Swings:**

1.  When there is a good indication that their son or daughter has a mood or sleep disorder or a Cyclothymic Disorder, parent(s) and child or teen are immediately referred to a treating child psychiatrist. A psychological evaluation, report and letter are faxed to this medical professional outlining psychological assessment, therapy procedures used, observations, and diagnostic impressions. The psychologist will state his reason for this referral and recommendations for treatment.

    When their son or daughter has mood swings, shows frequent anger towards others at home or school, we want to begin medical treatment with a low dose of medication to treat possible hypomanic mood and erratic sleep patterns. Such erratic sleep will encourage difficulty getting started in the mornings at home and at school. It is frequently necessary to begin medical treatment before counseling and therapy can be effective!

2.  In therapy, the son or daughter can begin specific individual therapy using the guide, *The Skill Streaming the Elementary School Child* (Research Press) as a guide to role play and practice social skills with the therapist, and later with the parent present. This

guide was written for use in Elementary Schools to teach small groups of children prosocial skills. This program is designed to help "behavior disordered children" who deal with events in an immature manner, with aggressive behavior, or with withdrawal. The authors believe these specific social skills can help all children.

There is an adolescent version of this guide to use with teenagers entitled: *Skill-streaming the Adolescent: A Structured Learning Approach to Teaching Prosocial Skills* by Goldstein etal., 1980. This guide provides wonderful detail on how to be a group trainer, and on the use of role playing and modeling both beginning and advanced social skills. Specific social skills are described in steps and role play situations at home, school or with peers are suggested, or practiced.

With mood disordered, impatient, restless children, adult mentors are encouraged to be aware of need for medical treatment to manage and prevent mood swings. The Cyclothymic student will need more hands-on activity and more movement, rhythmic, and musical activity and media to be motivated in such skill training groups. Yoga and the practice of Tai Chi can be incorporated in group activity to induce emotional, physical calm and relaxation along with balance in movement.

3.  Teenagers who are impatient and lack reading skills are motivated with the use of the Talking, Feeling, and Doing Game where they spin the wheel and count the moves. They proceed to pick up a Talking, Doing or Feeling card, read it slowly, and do what it says. The therapist models and mentors gentle, careful efforts at sounding out words. She shares examples of situations and feelings she has experienced. 'Have you ever had this happen to you and feel this way?', can be a helpful prompt.

The therapist can then use this game to ask therapeutic questions: "Have you ever felt this way recently?" (ie., angry, sad). "What was the circumstance?", or "what happened?" "Do you ever remember doing this with someone?" Perhaps someone has called them names or hit or pushed them. The student is encouraged to share their feelings and how they coped with the situation.

4.  The Feelings Wheel Game with its dice and playing piece is a brief game that young people enjoy. The therapist and teenager take turns sharing feelings they have experienced and telling or describing when and where they experienced this feeling. When the student observes the adult mentor share feelings in a calm, comfortable manner, they learn that there are a wide variety of feelings, and that it is normal to have them and to talk about them. (Leben, Acquaro, 1992).

5.  Teenagers especially appreciate The Coping Skills Game as this teaches practical skills they can use during the week, both at school and at home. We take turns reading Coping skill cards or Situation cards and answering questions. "Have you had a time when you fell and got hurt? How did you handle it?" (The Coping Skills Game, 1996).

**How do I get my children or moody teenager to cooperate?**
**He and she refuse to do chores or help around the house.**

This question frequently comes up with mood-disordered children. When parents remarry, this refusal to help can become a center of conflict with stepchildren.

It is best to start routines, chores, and responsibilities for "cleaning up" and "putting things away" at an early age. Positive habits can be established and reinforced more easily. Give clear, short instructions and post signs of family rules and what the rewards and consequences are for helping and failing to help.

"When you put away your toys and books and hang up your clothes and towels the next two days, we will go out for a dessert." "We will pick up a movie for Friday night and make popcorn, when everyone does their chores this week, and makes sure that their dirty clothes are put in the hamper in the laundry room."

"We will post a chart on the refrigerator listing your chores for the week and how many points you can earn for each chore. "We will add points on Friday evening or Saturday morning and, your father and I will talk with you about your privileges for the weekend and the allowance you earned."

When our girls neared the age of 12, we were more specific as to what behaviors we expected. Chores were spelled out and, we had family team meetings to discuss rules and responsibilities and how everyone helped-out. Teenagers require a different approach. A brief meeting with your teenager to review rules, to have them share ideas on how to best get chores and laundry done is helpful. Find out what bugs your teenager and what is seen as unfair, can be helpful in removing a blockage to helpful behavior.

Keep words to a minimum and avoid lecturing. Listen to feelings and consider what may be bothering your daughter or son. When your son or daughter feels heard, she will more likely want to help.

## Summary:

1.  Have your child's or teen's doctor and treatment provider take a thorough family medical and mental health history so that they may have a clear picture of what may influence your son or daughter's moods, behavior, and sleep patterns.

2.  When a diagnosis is given to treat your child, ask more questions and do more reading and research. Particularly ask questions about medications prescribed, their dosages, their side effects and their interactions with other drugs and medications. When the medication does not seem to help within 3 months, more questions need to be asked about diagnosis and medication used.

3.  Mood and sleep disorders are complex and children's biochemistry, neurobiology, nutritional needs, and gastro-intestinal health are complex. It takes time for doctors, treatment specialists, parents to figure out what contributes to the behavior, mood, sleep and substance abuse problems of children and teenagers. Evaluation

and treatment steps need to be taken carefully and in well planned steps to rule out problems and to rule in solutions.

4.  Be sure your child is included in the assessment and treatment planning of her or his problem. They should be answering questions, writing answers, drawing, and helping to find solutions. When they tell us a medication hurts their stomach, we need to listen. We need to listen to our sons and daughters however they explain their problem: by a checklist, by a poem or drawing, through a test, a game, or working with a sand tray.

5.  Violent and suicidal behavior: The two shooters at Columbine High School expressed themselves by shooting guns and making bomb material in the family basement. One was treated with an antidepressant, and they avoided others. No one was watching or listening to them. They shot others and killed themselves. Such students need to be engaged in social activities and emotional expression in group formats at an early age. Then their community can observe their healthy adaptative behavior or their maladaptive behavior at earlier ages. These families may be redirected, or family members may be medically treated effectively, earlier to prevent tragic outcomes.

6.  Adults, parents, teenagers, pre-teens need to become students of suicidal behavior. Coursework on mood, sleep disorders, suicidal and aggressive behavior, and nutrition and healthy exercise should be required for all middle and high school students. Books, like *People Making* by Virgina Satir and *Learned Optimism* by Martin Seligman, PhD can be made a central part of a human relations, family psychology course at school. Teenagers and parents need to examine such works as *Violent Attachments* by Reid Meloy, PhD. to understand violence in relationships and *Tragedy in Aurora: The Culture of Mass Shootings in America* by Tom Diaz to grasp what is behind violent behavior in America. (Meloy, 1992; Diaz, 2019).

The sooner students and their families understand what makes families work well and what makes lives better, the better for schools and communities. God bless America. May God protect children and families during these difficult months and times.

John A. Paulus, PhD

8/22/2020

# REFERENCES

Achenbach TM: *Manual for the Child Behavior Checklist/4-18 (CBCL Ages 4-18) and 1991 Profile.* Burlington: University of Vermont Department of Psychiatry. (1991).

Akiskal, Hagop S. (Editor), Tohen, Mauricio (Editor) *Bipolar Psychopharmacotherapy: Caring for the Patient.* (2011).

Akiskal, Hagop S. "Temperament, mood disorder and human nature: toward an Integration of psychological medicine and evolutionary biology." *Annals of General Psychiatry,* Assessment Chapter – (TEMPS), 5, Article number: S51 (2006).

Akiskal H.S., Akiskal, KK, eds: "TEMPS: Temperament Evaluation of Memphis, Pisa Paris, and San Diego (Special Issue) *J Affect Disord.* 85 (2005): 1-242.

Akiskal, H.S., Mendlowicz, M.V., Jean-Louis, G., Rapaport, M.H., Kelsoe, J.R., Gillin, J.C., Smith, T.L. "TEMPS-A: validation of a short version of a self-rated instrument designed to measure variations in temperament." *Journal of Affective Disorders,* 85 (2005): 45-52.

Akiskal, HS, Bourgeois, M L, Angst, J, Post, R, Moller, H-J, Hirschfeld, R "Re-evaluating the prevalence of and diagnostic composition within the broad clinical spectrum of bipolar disorders." *Journal of Affective Disorders* 59 (2000): S5-S30.

Akiskal, H.S., Pinto, O. "The evolving bipolar spectrum prototypes I, II, III and IV." *Psychiatric Clin North Am.* 22 (1999): 517-534. [Pub Med].

Akiskal, HS, Hantouch, EG, Bourgeois, M, Azorin, JM, Duchene, LC, "Gender, temperament, and the clinical picture in dysphoric mania: findings from a French National Study (EPIMAN)." *Journal of Affective Disorders.* 50, Issues 2-3 (1 September 1998): 175-186.

Akiskal and Malya, 1987. "Criteria for the "soft" bipolar spectrum: treatment implications." *Psychopharmacol Bull. 23(1)* (1987): *68-73.*

Akiskal, H.S. etal.,. "Cyclothymic temperamental disorders." *Psychiatr. Clin North Am* 2 (1979): 527-554.

Akiskal, H.S., Downs, J. "Affective Disorders in the Referred Children & Younger Siblings of Manic-depressives.". *Archives Gen Psychiatry* 42 (1985): 996-1003.

Akiskal, HS. "The Bipolar Spectrum: New Concepts in Classification and Diagnosis."In Grinspoon, L., editor *Psychiatry Update: The American Psychiatric Association Annual Review*, Volume 2. Washington D.C.: American Psychiatric Press. (1983): 271-292.

Algorta, G.P., etal., "Suicidality in pediatric bipolar disorder: predictor or outcome of family processes and mixed mood presentation?" *Bipolar Disord* 13 (1) (2011 Feb): 76-86.

Algorta, G.P., et al., "An Inexpensive Family Index of Risk for Mood Issues Improves Identification of Pediatric Bipolar Disorder." *Psychological Assessment* (2012, July 16).

Paula Alhola and Pavi Polo-Kantola. "Sleep deprivation: Impact on cognitive Performance." *Neuropsychiatr Dis Treat* (2007 Oct) 3(5): 553-567.

Maria Almond, "Depression and Inflammation: Examining the Link," *Curr Psychiatry,* 6, no.12 (2013): 24-32.

Angst, J. "The emerging epidemiology of hypomania and bipolar II disorder." *J. Affect. Disorder.* 50. (1998): 143-151.

Angst, J. "The bipolar spectrum." *Br J Psychiatry.* 190 (2007): 189-191.

Aronen ET, etal., "Sleep and psychiatric symptoms in school age children." *J Am Acad Child Adolesc Psychiatry* 39 (2000): 502-508.

Azorin, J.M., et al., H S. 2010 "Suicidal behavior in a French cohort of major depressive Patients: characteristics of attempters and nonattempters." *J Affect. Disord.* (2010): 87-94.

Baiden, P., et al., "Investigating the association between age at first alcohol use and suicidal ideation among high school students : Evidence from youth risk behavior surveillance system." *Journal of Affective Disorders* 242 (2019): 60-67.

Aaaron T. Beck. *Beck Anxiety Inventory.* San Antonia, Texas: Pearson Assessments. (1990, 1993).

Benazzi, F., Akiskal HS. "Delineating bipolar II mixed states in the Ravenna-San Diego collaborative study: the relative prevalence and diagnostic significance of hypomanic features during major depressive episodes." *J Affect Disord.* 67 (2001): 115-122.

Berman, A.L. "Adolescent Suicide: Issues and challenges." *Seminars in Adolescent Medicine*, 2 (1986a): 269-277.

Berman, A.L. "Suicide interventions in schools: Critical reflections." In A.A. Leenars & S. Wenckstern (Eds.), *Suicide Prevention in Schools* (1990b): *243-255.* Washington: Hemisphere Publishing Co.

Berman, A.L. & Jobes, D.A. *Youth suicide.* In B. Bonger (ed.), "Suicide: Guidelines for assessment, management, and treatment." (1992): *84-105.* New York: Oxford University Press.

Berman, A.L., Jobes, D.A., and Silverman, M.M.: *Adolescent Suicide: Assessment and Intervention.* Washington, DC, American Psychological Association, 2005.

Berne, Eric. *Games People Play.* New York, NY: Ballantine Books, 1967.

Biederman J: "Resolved: mania is mistaken for ADHD in pre-pubertal children." *J Am Acad Child Adolesc Psychiatry* 37 (1998): 1096-1098.

Bieler, Henry G., M.D. *Food is Your Best Medicine.* (New York, NY: Ballantine Books, 1965).

Child Symptom Inventory – 4: Parent Checklist. (Stony Brook, NY: Checkmate Plus LTD, 1994).

Conners' Rating Scales : CPRS-48. (North Tonawanda, NY : Multi-Health Systems., Inc., 1989).

Copeland, Mary Ellen. *The Depression Workbook.* (Oakland, California: New Harbinger Publications, 1992).

Endicott V., Spitzer, RL. "A diagnostic interview: the Schedule for Affective Disorders and Schizophrenia." *Arch Gen Psychiatry* 1978, 35: 837-848.

Fields, BW, Fristad, MA. "Assessment of Childhood Bipolar Disorder." *Clinical Psychology: Science and Practice.* 2009; 16(2): 166-181.

Fieve, Ronald R. *Moodswing,* Second Revised and Expanded Edition. (New York: Bantam Books, 1989).

Fife, Bruce. *The Coconut Ketogenic Diet.* (*Colorado Springs, CO: Piccadilly Books Ltd., 2019*).

Fristad, Mary A., et al., "Psychoeducation: A Promising Intervention Strategy for Families of Children and Adolescents with Mood Disorders." *Contemporary Family Therapy* 18(3), (September 1996).

Garfinkel, B.D., & Golombek, H. "Suicidal behavior in adolescence." In H. Golombek and B.D. Garfinkel (Eds.), *The Adolescent and Mood Disturbance.* New York: International Universities Press (1983).

Ghaemi, S. Nassir "Bipolar Spectrum: A review of the concept and a vision for the future." *Psychiatry Investig.* 10(3) (2013 Sept): 218-224.

Goldstein, A., Sprafkin, R., Gershaw, N., Klein, P. *Skill-streaming the Adolescent: A Structured Learning Approach to Teaching Prosocial Skills.* Champaign, Illinois: Research Press Company (1980).

Gregory, Christina. *Bipolar Spectrum Disorder: An Overview of the Soft Bipolar Spectrum. (2017).* (https://www.psycom.net.)

Hammill, Donald J., Brown, Virginia L., Larsen, Stephen C., Wiederholt, J. Lee (1994) *Test of Adolescent and Adult Language, Third Edition (TOAL-3).* Austin, Texas: pro-ed.

Hantouche, E.G., Angst, Jules, Akiskal, Hagop S. "Factor Structure of Hypomania: interrelationship with cyclothymia and the soft bipolar spectrum." *Journal of Affective Dis*, Vol. 73, Issues 1-2, January 2003, pages 39-47.

Robert M.A. Hirschfeld. *The Mood Questionnaire.* Galveston, Texas: University of Texas Medical Branch, Department of Psychiatry. (2000).

http:/www.doctoroz.com/videos/alzheimers-diabetes-brain.

Jacobsen, FM. "Low-dose valproate: a new treatment for cyclothymia, mild rapid cycling disorders, and premenstrual syndrome." *J Clin Psychiatry.* 1993 June; 54(6), 229-34.

K12Reader.com (2011) Grade – 5th Grade Spelling List Worksheets at http://www.k12reader.com. Copyright 2011 K12Reader.com

Kovacs, Maria (1992) *Children's Depression Inventory: CDI Manual.* North Tonawanda, NY: Multi-Health Systems.

Kunjufu, J. *Countering the conspiracy to destroy black boys: Vol. 3.* Chicago, Illinois: African American Images (1990).

David Lachar. *Personality Inventory for Children (PIC)* WPS: Torrance, CA. (1982).

J.W. Lee etal., "Neuro-inflammation Induced by Lipopolysaccharide Causes Cognitive Impairment through Enhancement of Beta-Amyloid Generation." *J. Neuroinflamm. 5 (August 29, 2008): 37, doi: 10.1186/1742-2094-5-37.*

Anna V. Lunde et al., "The Relationship of Bulimia and Anorexia Nervosa with Bipolar Disorder and Its Temperamental Foundations.", *Journal of Affective Disorders.* 115, Issue 3 (June 2009): 309-314.

*Susan L. McElroy et al.,* "Comorbidity of bipolar and eating disorders: distinct or related disorders with shared dysregulations?" *Journal of Affective Disorders, 86, Issues 2-3, (June 2005): 107-127.*

*Mayo Clinic: "Diabetes: What's the Connection between Diabetes and Depression: How Can I Cope If I have both?" Mayo Clinic, accessed January 12, 2015, http://www.mayoclinic.org/diseases-conditions/diabetes/expert-answers/Diabetes-and-depression/faq-20057904.*

McGinnis, E., Goldstein, A. *Skill-streaming the Elementary School Child: A Guide for Teaching Prosocial Skills.* (Champaign, Illinois : Research Press, 1984).

Mechri, A., et al., "Association between cyclothymic temperament and clinical predictors of bipolarity in recurrent depressive patients." *J. Affect Disord.* 132, (2011): 285-288.

Meloy, J. Reid (1992). *Violent Attachments.* (North Vale, New Jersey: Jason Aranson Inc., 1992).

Millon, T., Green, C.J., Meagher Jr., R.B. *Millon Adolescent Personality Inventory.* (New York City, NY: Pearson North America, 1986).

Millon, T., Tringone, R., Millon, C., Grossman, S. *Millon Pre-Adolescent Clinical Inventory (M-PACI)*. (New York City: NY: Pearson North America 2005).

Millon, T., Millon, C., Davis., R., Grossman S. *Millon Adolescent Clinical Inventory (MACI)*. (New York,City: NY: Pearson North America, 2006).

National Institute of Mental Health (NIMH) *"Bipolar Disorder"*. *http://www.nimh.nih.gov/publicat/bipolar.cfm. 5/13/2004*.

National Institute of Mental Health (NIMH) Mood chart. Rockvile, MD. https://www.nimh.gov/site-info/contact-nimh.

*Nelson-Denny Reading Test.* (Itasca, Ill.: Riverside Publishing, 1993).

NICHQ Vanderbilt Assessment Scale – Parent Informant. American Academy of Pediatrics and National Initiative for Children's Healthcare Quality. (2002).

Oaklander, Violet. *Windows to Our Children.* (Highland, NY: The Gestalt Journal Press, 1998).

Papolos, Demetri F., M.D. and Papolos, Janice. *The Bipolar Child: The Definitive Reassuring Guide to Childhood's Most Misunderstood Disorder* (New York: Broadway Books, 1999, 2002 (hardback), 2007 (soft cover)).

Papolos, Demitri, M.D., and Papolos, Janice. *Overcoming Depression*, Third Edition. (New York: HarperPerennial, 1997).

Paulus, John A. *Family factors and individual coping as predictors of urban middle school competence*: Dissertation, The Ohio State University, (Ann Arbor, Mich: UMI Dissertation Information Service., 1991).

Perlmutter, David. *Brain Maker: The Power of Gut Microbes to Heal and Protect Your Brain- for Life.* (New York: Little, Brown and Company, 2015)

Perlmutter, David. *Grain Brain: The Surprising Truth About Wheat, Carbs, and Sugar – Your Brain's Silent Killers.* (New York: Little, Brown and Company, 2013).

Giulio Perugi, et al., "Cyclothymia reloaded: A reappraisal of the most misconceived affective disorder", *Journal of Affective Disorders* 183 (2015): 119-133.

Giulio Perugi, et al., "Bulimia nervosa in atypical depression: The mediating role cyclothymic temperament", *Journal of Affective Disorders.* 92, Issue 1, (May 2006): 91-97.

Popper, Charles, Ph.D. "In Diagnosing Bipolar Disorder vs. ADHD: A Pharmacological Point of View." *The Link* 13 (1996).

Preston, John, PsyD., O'Neal, John, MD, and Talaga, Mary C., R.Ph., M.A. *Child and Adolescent Clinical Psychopharmacology Made Simple, 3rd edition.* (Oakland, CA: New Harbinger Publications, 2010).

Preston, John, PsyD., O'Neal, John H., MD, and Talaga, Mary C., Pharm., R.Ph., M.A. *Handbook of Clinical Psychopharmacology for Therapists, 8th edition* (Oakland, CA.: New Harbinger Publications, Inc., 2017).

Quinn, Colleen A., MS. and Fristad, Mary A., Ph.D. "Defining and Identifying Early Onset Bipolar Spectrum Disorder". *Current Psychiatry Reports 6 (2004)* :101-107.

Reuben, David. *The Save Your Life Diet.* (New York: Ballantine Books, 1975).

Reynolds, W.M. *Suicide Adolescent Depression Scale.* (Odessa, FLA: Psychological Assessment Resources, Inc., 1987)

R.O. Roberts, et al., "Relative Intake of Macronutrients Impacts Risk of Mild Cognitive Impairment or Dementia, *"Journal of Alzheimer's Disease* 32, no. 2 (2012): 329-39.

Satir, Virginia. *People Making.* (London: SouvenirPress, 1990).

Schneider, Mary F. *CAST: Children's Apperceptive Story-Telling Test.* (Austin, Texas: PRO-ED, 1989).

Seligman, Martin E.P. *The Optimistic Child: A Proven Program to Safeguard Children Against Depression and Build Lifelong Resilience.* (New York: Houghton Mifflin, 2007).

Shea, S.C.: *The Practical Art of Suicide Assessment.* (New York: NY: John Wiley & Sons, Inc., 2002).

Shea, Shawn Christopher, M.D. "Suicide Assessment Part 2: Uncovering Suicidal Intent Using the Chronological Assessment of Suicide Events (CASE Approach)." *Psychiatric Times.com* (Vol. No. December 21, 2009).

Smith, LA, Cornelius, VR, Azorin, JM etal., "Valproate for the treatment of Acute bipolar depression: systematic review and meta-analysis." *J Affect Dis* 22: (2010): 1-9.

Stanley, E.J. and Barter, J.T. (1970). *Adolescent Suicidal Behavior.* In Am. Journal Of Orthopsychiatry, Vol 40: 87-96.

Steenari, Maija-Riikka, Vuontela, V, Paavonen, EJ, Carlson S, Fjallber, M, and Aronen, E. "Working Memory and Sleep in 6- to 13-Year Old Schoolchildren" *J Am. Acad. Child Adolesc. Psychiatry*, 2003, 42 (1) 85-92.

Stokes, A. (1990). "Relationship among level of cognitive development, gender, chronological age, and mathematics achievement. *"Journal of Negro Education*, 59(3), 299-314.

*Test of Variables of Attention (TOVA).* Langley, WA. The TOVA Company. (1991).

*The Talking, Feeling and Doing Game.* Childswork/Childsplay. Bohemia, NY. (1973).

Tomba, E., et al., Clinical configuration of Cyclothymic disturbances. *Journal of Affective Disorders,* 139 (2012): 244-249.

Anna Van Meter, et al., "Examining the Validity of Cyclothymic Disorder in a youth sample." *J Affect Disorder, (2011, July); 132(1-2) 55-63.*

Anna Van Meter et al., "Cyclothymic disorder: A Critical Review." *Clinical Psychology Review,* Volume 32, Issue 4, (June 2012), 229-243.

Verhoeven, W.M.A, Tuinier, S. "Cyclothymia or unstable mood disorder? A systematic treatment evaluation with valproic acid." *Journal of Applied Research in Intellectual Disabilities.* Vol 14, Issue 2: December 2001.

Walker, Peter. *How Cycling Can Save the World* (New York: Tarcher Perigree/Penguin Random House, 2017).

*Wechsler Intelligence Scale for Children – Third Edition.* Minneapolis, Minn.: Pearson Assessment. (1991). (PsychCorp/Harcourt Assessment, Inc. merged with Pearson in Jan., 2008).

*Wechsler Intelligence Scale for Children – Fourth Edition (WISC-IV).* Minneapolis, Minn.: Pearson Assessment. (2003).

Werner, E.E. & Smith, R.S. *Vulnerable but invincible: A longitudinal study of resilient children and youth.* New York: Adams.Bannister. Cox. (1982).

Whybrow, Peter C., M.D. *A Mood Apart: Depression, Mania, and Other Afflictions of the Self.* New York: Basic Books. (2015).

*Woodcock Johnson Tests of Achievement III (WJ-III).* Itasca, Ill.: Riverside Press. (2001).

Yee, A.M., Algorta, G.P., Youngstrom, EA., Findling, R.L. Birmaher, B., Fristad, M. A., and the LAMS Group. "Unfiltered administration of the YMRS and CDRS-R in a clinical sample of children". *J Clin Child Adolesc Psychol.* (2015). Nov-Dec; 44(6): 992-1007.

Youngstrom, EA. "Definitional issues in bipolar disorder across the life cycle." *Clinical Psychology Science Practice.* (2009) 16(2): 140-160.

Youngstrom, EA, Duax, J. "Evidence based assessment of pediatric bipolar disorder, Part 1: Base rate and family history." *Journal of the American Academy of Child and Adolescent Psychiatry,* (2005) 44: 712-717.

Zucker, Robert. Alcoholism: *Clinical & Experimental Research*, April, 2004.